THE PILLARS
of
CHRISTIAN
CHARACTER

THE PILLARS

of

CHRISTIAN CHARACTER

---

*The Basic Essentials
of a Living Faith*

JOHN F. MACARTHUR

CROSSWAY BOOKS • WHEATON, ILLINOIS
A DIVISION OF GOOD NEWS PUBLISHERS

Library of Congress Cataloging-in-Publication Data
MacArthur, John, 1939-
    The pillars of Christian character / John F. MacArthur
       p.   cm.
    Includes indexes.
    ISBN 0-89107-950-5 (tpb : alk. paper)
    1. Virtues.   2. Character.   3. Christian Life.   I. Title.
    BV4630.M25   1998
    179'.9—dc21   98-16146
                                              CIP

11	10	09	08	07	06	05	04	03	02	01	00	99	98
15	14	13	12	11	10	9	8	7	6	5	4	3	2	1

CONTENTS

INTRODUCTION

If you ever visit London, you'll have no trouble spotting St. Paul's Cathedral. It's considered to be among the ten most beautiful buildings in the world, and it dominates the city's skyline. The venerable structure stands as a monument to its creator—astronomer and architect Sir Christopher Wren. While St. Paul's is his best-known achievement, an interesting story is connected with a lesser-known building of his design.

Wren was given charge of designing the interior of the town hall in Windsor, just west of central London. His plans called for large columns to support the high ceiling. When construction was complete, the city fathers toured the building and expressed concern over one problem: the pillars. It wasn't that they minded the use of pillars—they just wanted more of them.

Wren's solution was as devilish as it was inspired. He did exactly as he was told and installed four new pillars, thus meeting the demands of his critics. Those extra pillars remain in the Windsor town hall to this day, and they aren't difficult to identify. They are the ones that support no weight and, in fact, never even reach the ceiling. They're fakes. Wren installed the pillars to serve only one purpose—to look good. They are ornamental embellishments built to satisfy the eye. In terms of supporting the building and fortifying the structure, they are as useful as the paintings that hang on the walls.

While it saddens me to say this, I believe many churches have constructed a few decorative pillars of their own, especially in the lives of their people. In an effort to renew the church and make it work better, many leaders have implemented attractive styles of worship and teaching, along with "innovative" organizational formats designed to attract more people to the church. *Substance* has been replaced by *shadow*. *Content* is out—*style* is in. *Meaning* is out—*method* is in. The church may look right, but it bears little weight.

That trend is perhaps most evident in an area especially close to my heart—the teaching of God's Word. Too many churches today have forgotten that their main purpose is a simple one. As "the church of the living God," they are to be "the pillar and support of the truth" (1 Tim. 3:15). Instead, they have built a façade that offers no support, bears little weight, and falls far short of reaching the heights God designed for the church and wants it to reach.

What results is the existence of phony, decorative pillars in the lives of the people, which ultimately delude them into a false sense of their salvation and spiritual maturity. They never come to grips with the real issue—the need to transform their old, sinful heart attitudes into new, scriptural ones. In nearly thirty years of ministry at Grace Community Church I have learned that if the spiritual attitudes of the people are right—as a result of careful, long-term, biblical teaching—the church's organizational structure, form, and style become far less important.

A healthy life for the church comes only from the proper spiritual attitudes of its members (cf. Deut. 30:6; Matt. 22:37; Mark 12:32-34; Heb. 10:22). The apostle Paul's earnest desire, for which he labored and prayed so diligently, was that Jesus Christ be fully formed in the lives of those he ministered to: "I am again in labor until Christ is formed in you" (Gal. 4:19). He expanded that concept when he encouraged the Colossians to "let the word of Christ richly dwell within you, with all wisdom teaching and admonishing one another with psalms and hymns and spiritual songs, singing with thankfulness in your hearts to God" (3:16). It's the believer's inner person that God wants to work on. Therefore, transformed lives should be the goal of all pastors and church leaders. Every ministry and worship activity they lead ought to motivate their people to think biblically.

It is my desire that this book would awaken you and encourage your heart toward the key spiritual attitudes that will motivate and transform your life from the inside out. With that in mind we will discuss thirteen fundamental attitudes, or pillars if you will, of Christian character that Scripture teaches all genuine followers of Christ must possess and be continually developing. It is not an exhaustive list, but each attitude is essential for mature Christian behavior.

The first five chapters define, explain, and illustrate the basic Christian pillars of faith, obedience, humility, love, and unity. Chapter 6 is a reminder that spiritual growth is a command, not an option. Chapters 7—9 will encourage you to display the attitudes of forgiveness, joy, and thankfulness at all times, even when circumstances make it difficult to do so. Chapter 10 is a discussion of spiritual strength, focusing on the pictures of a strong Christian in 2 Timothy 2. In chapter 11, we'll consider some principles of self-discipline and practical ways to apply them. Chapter 12 views the nature of true worship, centering on Jesus' teaching to the Samaritan woman in John 4. Finally, in chapter 13 we'll make a careful study of the attitude of Christian hope and will see that it is a wonderful source of optimism and reassurance.

Without question the crucial issue in living the Christian life is the condition of your heart. Are you understanding and applying the fundamental pillars of Christian character that God's Word so clearly outlines? The apostle Paul writes this excellent summary of how a godly attitude applies to everyday living: "Slaves, be obedient to those who are your masters according to the flesh, with fear and trembling, in *the sincerity of your heart, as to Christ*; not by way of eyeservice, as men-pleasers, but as slaves of Christ, *doing the will of God from the heart*"

(Eph. 6:5-7, emphasis added). It is my sincere prayer that "doing the will of God from the heart" will become an abiding reality in your life as a result of this study.

1

THE STARTING POINT: GENUINE FAITH

In a commonplace way, faith or trust underlies how everyone lives. We drink water for various reasons and trust that it has been safely processed. We trust that the food we purchase at the supermarket or that we eat at a restaurant is uncontaminated. We routinely cash or deposit checks, even though the paper they're written on has no intrinsic value. We put our trust in the reliability of the company or person who issues the check. We sometimes submit to the surgeon's scalpel, even though we don't have any expertise in medical procedures. Every day we exercise an innate faith in someone or something.

WHAT IS SPIRITUAL FAITH?

In a similar way, when you have spiritual faith you willingly accept basic ideas and act on many things you don't understand. However, your spiritual faith does not operate innately, as natural faith does. Natural trust accompanies natural birth, and spiritual trust is a direct result of spiritual birth. Paul's familiar words in Ephesians 2:8 remind us, "For by grace you have been saved through faith; and that not of yourselves, it is the gift of God."

A modern-language version of one of the older church confessions (closely patterned after the Westminster Confession) provides this clear, doctrinal description of practical faith for the believer:

By faith a Christian believes everything to be true that is made known in the Word, in which God speaks authoritatively. He also perceives in the Word a degree of excellence superior to all other writings, indeed to all things that the world contains. The Word shows the glory of God as seen in His various attributes, the excellence of Christ in His nature and in the offices He bears, and the power and perfection of the Holy Spirit in all the works in which He is engaged. In this way the Christian is enabled to trust himself implicitly to the truth thus believed, and to render service according to the different requirements of the various parts of Scripture. To the commands he yields obedience; when he hears threatenings he trembles; as for the divine promises concerning this life and that which is to come, he embraces them. But the principal acts of saving faith relate in the first instance to Christ as the believer accepts, receives and rests upon Him alone for justification, sanctification, and eternal life; and all by virtue of . . . grace. (*A Faith to Confess: The Baptist Confession of Faith of 1689* [Sussex, England: Carey Publications, 1975], 37)

So the first foundational pillar God's people must have is spiritual faith, or trust in God. And that attitude will not grow and develop unless individual believers come to know God better and better. That truth is exemplified throughout Scripture. Here are just a few prominent examples:

• *Moses*—"The LORD is my strength and song, and He has become my salvation; this is my God, and I will praise Him; my father's God, and I will extol Him" (Exod. 15:2).

• *David*—"I love Thee, O LORD, my strength. The LORD is my rock and my fortress and my deliverer, my God, my rock, in whom I take refuge; my shield and the horn of my salvation, my stronghold. I call upon the LORD, who is worthy to be praised, and I am saved from my enemies" (Ps. 18:1-3).

• *Jeremiah*—"'The LORD is my portion,' says my soul, 'therefore I have hope in Him'" (Lam. 3:24).

• *Paul*—"For it is for this we labor and strive, because we have fixed our hope on the living God, who is the Savior of all men, especially of believers" (1 Tim. 4:10).

• *John*—"Whoever confesses that Jesus is the Son of God, God abides in him, and he in God. And we have come to know and have believed the love which God has for us" (1 John 4:15-16).

HABAKKUK'S EXAMPLE OF FAITH

For a more in-depth look at how biblical saints exemplified the attitude of faith, let's consider the case of the prophet Habakkuk. He ministered in the late seventh century B.C., during the last days of Assyria's power and the beginning days of Babylon's rule (about 625 B.C. to 600 B.C.). The situation in Habakkuk's day was similar to what Amos and Micah faced. Justice and faithfulness had basically disappeared from Judah, and there was much unchecked wickedness and violence throughout the land.

Why No Answer, God?

The opening of Habakkuk's prophecy, or sermon, reveals his frustration and lack of understanding of why God did not intervene in Judah's affairs and dramatically set things right:

> *How long, O LORD, will I call for help, and Thou wilt not hear? I cry out to Thee, "Violence!" Yet Thou dost not save. Why dost Thou make me see iniquity, and cause me to look on wickedness? Yes, destruction and violence are before me; strife exists and contention arises. Therefore, the law is ignored and justice is never upheld. For the wicked surround the righteous; therefore, justice comes out perverted.*
>
> —1:2-4

The prophet faced a real dilemma. He probably had already petitioned the Lord to either bring about a spiritual revival so all Judah would repent, or to judge the people for all their wickedness, violence, perversion of justice, and inattention to His law. But God was not doing either, and Habakkuk could not understand how He could observe the magnitude of Judah's evil and not act.

Why the Chaldeans?

But in the next passage God gives Habakkuk a most startling and unexpected answer:

> "Look among the nations! Observe! Be astonished! Wonder! Because I am doing something in your days—you would not believe if you were told. For behold, I am raising up the Chaldeans, that fierce and impetuous people who march throughout the earth to seize dwelling places which are not theirs. They are dreaded and feared. Their justice and authority originate with themselves. Their horses are swifter than leopards and keener than wolves in the evening. Their horsemen come galloping, their horsemen come from afar; they fly like an eagle swooping down to devour. All of them come for violence. Their horde of faces moves forward. They collect captives like sand. They mock at kings, and rulers are a laughing matter to them. They laugh at every fortress, and heap up rubble to capture it. Then they will sweep through like the wind and pass on. But they will be held guilty, they whose strength is their god."
>
> —1:5-11

God's revelation only intensified Habakkuk's bewilderment, because it was not what Habakkuk expected or wanted to hear. How could the Lord possibly use the Chaldeans, a pagan people who were much greater sinners than the Jews, to judge and punish His covenant people?

After all, throughout their history the Chaldeans were notorious for being a militaristic, aggressive people. They originated from the mountains of Kurdistan and Armenia, north of Iraq, and later established their own small territory in southern Babylonia at the head of the Persian Gulf. From the earliest days of Assyria's rule over the Babylonians, the Chaldeans were a source of opposition and irritation to the Assyrian kings. Eventually, the Chaldeans had a key role in overthrowing Assyria and establishing and expanding the new Babylonian Empire.

The Chaldeans worshiped nothing but their military prowess and were certainly ready to "heap up rubble" to capture Jerusalem. (In the ancient Middle East, the stone walls of a city or fort were scaled once invading troops piled rubble against the walls. That rubble formed a ramp upon which the soldiers could march up and into the city.) The Chaldeans were sinful, self-centered, and ruthless, and Habakkuk could not understand how God could choose a far worse people than Judah to be the agents for chastening His people.

Solving the Dilemma

Habakkuk's puzzling dilemma definitely could not be solved with human wisdom. Because he did not understand God's plan, the prophet looked to his theology: "Art Thou not from everlasting, O LORD, my God, my Holy One? We will not die. Thou, O LORD, hast appointed them to judge; and Thou, O Rock, hast established them to correct" (1:12).

At the height of his confusion, as he was sinking into the quicksand of his dilemma and realizing that he could not answer his questions alone, Habakkuk wisely reached out for what he knew to be true about God. First, he recognized that God is eternal and has existed from eternity past and will exist into eternity future. Habakkuk was reminding himself that the troubles he and the nation faced were really just part of a short period in world history. The Lord was far greater than any small moment in time, problems and all, and He knew all along how everything fit into His eternal plan.

The prophet underscored his opening words by addressing God as "O LORD, my God, my Holy One." The term for *Lord* here is the Hebrew *adoni*, which means "sovereign ruler." Habakkuk knew that God was and is in charge of all circumstances—He is omnipotent, and nothing ever gets beyond His control. Furthermore, Habakkuk acknowledged that God is holy—He does not make mistakes, and He perfectly carries out His program.

Habakkuk needed to find a secure spiritual footing in his under-standing of who God is and what He does. Therefore he could reassure himself that "We will not die." He knew God would remain faithful and not destroy Judah, since He had to fulfill the promised covenant He made with Abraham, which guaranteed a kingdom, a future, and a salvation.

Habakkuk saw God's faithfulness and His person in the closing words of verse 12, "Thou, O LORD, hast appointed them [the Chaldeans] to judge; and Thou, O Rock, hast established them to correct." He now accepted the fact that God was too pure to approve or excuse evil and that His eyes could not favorably observe wickedness. Therefore, He had determined to punish the people of Judah, and He had sovereignly chosen the Chaldeans to mete out that punishment. Even though Habakkuk would not have chosen that method of judgment, he could now say with much greater assurance of faith than before, "I see and accept what's going on."

Faith Summarized and Applied

The essence of Habakkuk's grappling with faith's definition was determined when God told him, "Behold, as for the proud one, his soul is not right within him; but the righteous will live by his faith" (2:4). The final phrase of this verse is one of the most important statements in all of Scripture because it succinctly expresses the foundational doctrine of justification by faith. For that reason it eventually became—in its *King James* form, "The just shall live by faith"—one of the great Reformation mottoes.

Nineteenth-century Reformation historian J. H. Merle D'Aubigne describes Martin Luther's discovery of the crucial truth of Habakkuk 2:4 in this way:

> He [Luther] began his course by explaining the Psalms, and thence passed to the Epistle to the Romans. It was more particularly while meditating on this portion of Scripture that the light of truth penetrated his heart. In the retirement of his quiet cell, he used to consecrate

whole hours to the study of the divine Word, this epistle of the apostle Paul lying open before him. On one occasion, having reached the seventeenth verse of the first chapter, he read this passage from the prophet Habakkuk, "The just shall live by faith." This precept struck him. There is then for the just a life different from that of other men: and this life is the gift of faith. This promise, which he received into his heart as if God Himself had placed it there, unveiled to him the mystery of the Christian life and increased this life in him. Years after, in the midst of numerous occupations, he imagined he still heard these words: "The just shall live by faith." (*The Life and Times of Martin Luther* [1846; Chicago: Moody, 1978 edition], 46)

That occurred while Luther was a young professor teaching biblical theology at the University of Wittenberg in Germany in the early 1500s. The insight affected him so profoundly that a few years later he was prompted to compose the famous Ninety-five Theses and post them on the church door in Wittenberg. Those statements challenged the Roman Catholic Church to be more scriptural in some of its doctrines and practices. Notably, Luther took issue with the church's selling of indulgences to grant forgiveness of sins. He pointed out that such remission is granted freely and graciously by God, but only to those who come to Him in genuine repentance and faith. That soon led to a fuller development of the biblical doctrine of justification by faith and to the spread of the Protestant Reformation throughout much of Europe.

God's declaration to Habakkuk is also used in key passages in the New Testament. In addition to its pivotal usage in Romans 1:17, it is quoted two other times in the epistles: "Now that no one is justified by the Law before God is evident; for, 'The righteous man shall live by faith'" (Gal. 3:11); "But My righteous one shall live by faith; and if he shrinks back, My soul has no pleasure in him" (Heb. 10:38).

The prophet Habakkuk did not relegate the attitude of faith to

the theological realm only. He gives it a wonderful expression of prac-
ticality in the final three verses of his prophecy:

> *Though the fig tree should not blossom, and there be no fruit on*
> *the vines, though the yield of the olive should fail, and the fields*
> *produce no food, though the flock should be cut off from the fold,*
> *and there be no cattle in the stalls, yet I will exult in the LORD,*
> *I will rejoice in the God of my salvation. The LORD God is my*
> *strength, and He has made my feet like hinds' feet, and makes me*
> *walk on my high places.*
>
> —*3:17-19*

That language was very meaningful and familiar to the agricultural society of Habakkuk's audience. They knew the fig trees always
blossomed, the grape vines seemed never to fail, and the olive trees
were so sturdy and long-lasting that they would always produce a
good crop. It was inconceivable to them that the fields would stop
producing food and the livestock would cease having lambs and
calves.

The prophet is saying that even if the routine, ordinary, depend-
able parts of daily life quit functioning—if the whole world were
turned upside-down and backwards—he would still rejoice in God
and keep trusting in Him. Even when he didn't understand the circumstances, he still understood the person and work of God.

Habakkuk concludes by comparing his stability to that which
the Lord gives the mountain goat (the hind). As I've had the opportunity to fly close to mountains in Alaska, I've seen how mountain
goats behave. They will stand on the rugged, rocky edge of steep
cliffs, calm and confident, knowing that their hooves are safely and
securely anchored to the path. That's the kind of confidence God
gave Habakkuk and that He will give all believers. Even though we
might be on the precipice, completely puzzled in the face of an
unsolvable dilemma or an inescapable difficulty, the Lord can make
us like spiritual mountain goats who walk surefootedly over the high
places without fear of falling. None of life's precipices is too over-

whelming if we have the proper attitude of trust in God, as Habakkuk did.

FAITH POSSIBLE THROUGH CHRIST

In Galatians 2:20, the apostle Paul gives this testimony to the life of faith: "I have been crucified with Christ; and it is no longer I who live, but Christ lives in me; and the life which I now live in the flesh I live by faith in the Son of God, who loved me, and delivered Himself up for me." Paul is simply saying that he and all other genuine believers in Christ live their lives constantly trusting in the Savior. The apostle also said, "We walk by faith, not by sight" (2 Cor. 5:7). That means the Christian does not ultimately evaluate life through his natural senses, but through the eyes of faith. How could Paul be so confident that the Christian life could operate that way? Because of what he told the Philippians: "My God shall supply all your needs according to His riches in glory in Christ Jesus" (4:19). The real key to living a life of faith is the divine means supplied by the indwelling, powerful, ever-present Savior and Lord, Jesus Christ.

It's clear, then, that the first great Christian attitude, faith, begins at salvation and will characterize your entire Christian life. It is the foundational pillar on which to build your life, if you claim to love Jesus Christ. That was Paul's point in Romans 5:1-10:

Therefore having been justified by faith, we have peace with God through our Lord Jesus Christ, through whom also we have obtained our introduction by faith into this grace in which we stand; and we exult in hope of the glory of God. And not only this, but we also exult in our tribulations, knowing that tribulation brings about perseverance; and perseverance, proven character; and proven character, hope; and hope does not disappoint, because the love of God has been poured out within our hearts through the Holy Spirit who was given to us. For while we were still helpless, at the right time Christ died for the ungodly. For one will hardly die for a righteous man; though perhaps for the good man some-

one would dare even to die. But God demonstrates His own love toward us, in that while we were yet sinners, Christ died for us. Much more then, having been justified by His blood, we shall be saved from the wrath of God through Him. For if while we were enemies, we were reconciled to God through the death of His Son, much more, having been reconciled, we shall be saved by His life.

2

OBEDIENCE:
THE BELIEVER'S COVENANT

The perfect companion to faith is obedience. The final stanza of the familiar hymn "Trust and Obey" summarizes quite well the partnership these two foundational attitudes have: "Then in fellowship sweet we will sit at His feet, or we'll walk by His side in the way; what He says we will do, where He sends we will go—never fear, only trust and obey." The line "what He says we will do, where He sends we will go" gives us a simple definition of spiritual obedience. It basically means submitting to the Lord's commands, doing His will, based on what is so clearly revealed in Scripture.

FAITH AND OBEDIENCE INSEPARABLE

Jesus' Great Commission to the disciples indicates just how foundational the matter of obedience is for believers: "Go therefore and make disciples of all the nations, baptizing them in the name of the Father and the Son and the Holy Spirit, teaching them to observe all that I commanded you; and lo, I am with you always, even to the end of the age" (Matt. 28:19-20). While verse 19 involves proclaiming the Gospel, seeing people saved, and having them publicly profess their faith in Christ, verse 20 builds on the new converts' salvation experience. Disciplers, or any mature believers, will teach new Christians to obey God's commands in His Word and to submit to Him. The

Great Commission delineates the two great essentials of the sanctification process, or the believer's life in Christ—faith and obedience.

Obedience is so foundational that if it is not present in the life of one who claims to be a Christian, that person's faith ought to be questioned. This truth is emphasized more than once by the apostle John: "Jesus therefore was saying to those Jews who had believed in Him, 'If you abide in [obey] My Word, then you are truly disciples of Mine'" (John 8:31); "If you keep My commandments, you will abide in My love" (15:10). He reiterates the principle even more plainly in his first epistle: "And by this we know that we have come to know Him, if we keep His commandments. The one who says, 'I have come to know Him,' and does not keep His commandments, is a liar, and the truth is not in him" (1 John 2:3-4).

All who profess faith in Jesus Christ must also demonstrate that faith by obeying God's Word. Otherwise, their profession of saving faith is suspect. The obedience of a true believer will be unequivocal, uncompromising, not grudging, and from the heart. Obedience is therefore an integral part of one's salvation.

In fact, the apostle Peter describes salvation as an act of obedience: ". . . you have in obedience to the truth purified your souls for a sincere love of the brethren . . . for you have been born again not of seed which is perishable but imperishable, that is, through the living and abiding word of God" (1 Pet. 1:22-23). "The truth" is the Gospel, which in essence is a command to repent and believe in the Lord Jesus Christ (Mark 1:15). In the New Testament, the gospel message was always preached as a command (e.g., Matt. 3:2; 4:17; Mark 6:12; Luke 5:32; Acts 2:38; 3:19; 17:30; 26:20). Because it is a command, it calls for obedience, and all who are genuinely born again have new spiritual life because they heard the truth contained in Scripture, believed it, and obeyed it.

However, the moment of salvation involves more than an isolated act of obedience. When anyone places his trust in Christ's atoning work and receives His forgiveness of sins, he also acknowledges that the Savior is Lord and Master over his life. That means each believer has committed himself to a life of ongoing obedience, although initially he did not fully grasp all the implications of that commitment.

The reason we don't immediately understand all the ramifications of our commitment to Christ is that God, through the Holy Spirit, must first give us that sense of dedication. It does not originate with us, but the Spirit produces in our hearts the willingness to travel the pathway of obedience to God as servants of Jesus Christ. That's the process of sanctification, but it is only one phase of our salvation.

A well-rounded perspective on salvation and its fuller implications begins with a basic understanding of divine election. First Peter 1:1-2 describes believers as those "who are chosen according to the foreknowledge of God the Father." *Foreknowledge* is often misinterpreted. It does not mean all people have operated by their own will, with God as a neutral observer looking ahead from eternity past to see who would believe in Him and who would not and then choosing to save some and reject others. Instead, foreknowledge means that before anyone was born, God lovingly predetermined to intimately know some individuals and save them.

The Greek word for *foreknow* denotes a predetermined relationship, which is the same concept that defined God's plan to choose Israel from among all the other nations. He could have chosen a more prestigious and powerful country to proclaim His truth to the world, but He sovereignly predetermined to have a special, personal relationship with Israel (see Amos 3:2). Jesus spoke of this regarding believers when He said, "My sheep hear My voice, and I know them, and they follow Me" (John 10:27).

Election according to God's foreknowledge is the first phase of salvation. The Lord predetermined before the foundation of the world to have a close spiritual relationship with certain people, those who have believed or will yet believe the Gospel before the end of the age.

Peter's next phrase in verse 2, "by the sanctifying work of the Spirit," brings us again to sanctification, the present phase of salvation. That which was in the decree of God in eternity past (election) moved into time through the sanctifying work of the Holy Spirit. That means believers are saved by the agency of the Spirit: "Truly, truly, I say to you, unless one is born of water and the Spirit, he cannot enter into the kingdom of God" (John 3:5). So the Spirit's sanctifying work begins when we are saved. Sanctification includes being set apart from the control of sin, death, hell, and Satan and being enabled by the Holy Spirit to live an obedient life, conformed more and more to the image of Jesus Christ.

Living a life of obedience is the third and future phase of salvation, as indicated by Peter's statement, "that you may obey Jesus Christ and be sprinkled with His blood" (v. 2). The overarching purpose of redemption is that all believers would live the remainder of their lives walking in obedience to the Lord. The apostle Paul illuminates and sums up this future phase of salvation in Ephesians 2:10, "For we are His workmanship, created in Christ Jesus for good works, which God prepared beforehand, that we should walk in them."

A COVENANT OF OBEDIENCE

Peter's brief expression in 1 Peter 1:2, "and be sprinkled with His blood," presents us with an interesting interpretive challenge. The apostle's words are relevant to our discussion of salvation issues, but at first glance their meaning may seem a bit strange or obscure. The meaning, however, was clear to Peter's original audience, which included many converted Jews. He was referring to the following key passage from the Pentateuch and the graphic ceremony it depicts:

> *Then Moses came and recounted to the people all the words of the LORD and all the ordinances; and all the people answered with one voice, and said, "All the words which the LORD has spoken we will do!" And Moses wrote down all the words of the LORD. Then he arose early in the morning, and built an altar at the foot of the mountain with twelve pillars for the twelve tribes of Israel. And he sent young men of the sons of Israel, and they offered burnt offerings and sacrificed young bulls as peace offerings to the LORD. And Moses took half of the blood and put it in basins, and the other half of the blood he sprinkled on the altar. Then he took the book of the covenant and read it in the hearing of the people; and they said, "All that the LORD has spoken we will do, and we will*

be obedient!" So Moses took the blood and sprinkled it on the people, and said, "Behold the blood of the covenant, which the LORD has made with you in accordance with all these words."
                                                            —Exod. 24:3-8

As Exodus 24 begins, Moses has just recently received God's law (the Ten Commandments and many other ordinances) on Mount Sinai. Prior to the new Mosaic law, God had revealed His will and ways to His people in many different fashions. But from now on His will would be written down in absolute specifics—everything in the moral and ceremonial laws and all the laws of social and economic life.

After he came down from the mountain, Moses, with the Spirit's help, orally recounted God's massive law to the people. And they responded orally with one voice of public promise, basically saying, "We will obey all that we've heard." Thus began a covenant-making process between God and His people. God agreed, in the form of the Mosaic law, to provide the people with a set of standards for behavior that when violated would have certain moral and spiritual implications. The people agreed, in the form of their willing public vow, to obey God's words and follow the path of righteousness that His law now established.

Following his oral recitation of the law, Moses (presumably throughout the night) wrote down, under the Holy Spirit's inspiration, all those words of the law. Early the next morning he built an altar at the foot of Mount Sinai to publicly symbolize the sealing of the covenant made the previous day between God and the people. To represent everyone's participation, the altar's prominent feature consisted of twelve stone pillars (actually stacks of stones), one for each of the twelve tribes of Israel. To further signify everyone's solemn resolve to obey God's law, burnt offerings and peace offerings of young bulls were made in the presence of the Lord.

Next, Moses did quite a fascinating thing with all the blood that was produced as the young bulls were slaughtered and prepared for sacrifice. Half the blood remained in large basins, and the other half Moses splattered on the altar, which represented God. This splattering of the blood was the next demonstrable, symbolic step Moses took to ratify the covenant.

Then, as if to reinforce the importance of its contents, Moses allowed the people a second opportunity to hear the law by reading all of the words he had recorded the night before. The people of Israel responded exactly as they had to the previous recitation of the law: "All that the LORD has spoken we will do, and we will be obedient!" (v. 7).

Finally, Moses sealed the covenant made between God and the people by taking the blood from the basins and splattering it on the people. Blood was the physical demonstration that a commitment had been made between the parties. The blood on the altar symbolized God's agreement to reveal His law; the blood on the people symbolized their agreement to obey that law.

Thus the vivid symbolism of Exodus 24:3-8 is an excellent parallel to the statements about salvation in 1 Peter 1:2. When Peter says, "and be sprinkled with His blood," the apostle simply means that when a believer trusts Christ, he accepts His part of the new covenant. God allowed the prophet Ezekiel to foresee this principle: "Moreover, I will give you a new heart and put a new spirit within you; and I will remove the heart of stone from your flesh and give you a heart of flesh. And I will put My Spirit within you and cause you to walk in My statutes, and you will be careful to observe My ordinances" (Ezek. 36:26-27; cf. Jer. 31:33).

Thus salvation was and is a covenant of obedience. God offered His Word, His means of grace, His blessing and care, and we responded by promising to obey. It's as if the blood that was splattered on Christ, the perfect sacrifice, was then splattered on us because of our acceptance of His new covenant. What a wonderful picture that is.

OBEDIENCE IN PRACTICE

When we came to a saving faith in Jesus Christ, we entered a whole new realm of obedience. Prior to that, we had been obedient to the flesh, the world, and the devil and were controlled by all the various facets of sin. But as believers, we are now to be obedient to the righteousness of Christ.

Romans 6:16-18 reminds us of what our position is in Christ and therefore what kind of obedient attitude we must have:

Do you not know that when you present yourselves to someone as slaves for obedience, you are slaves of the one whom you obey, either of sin resulting in death, or of obedience resulting in righteousness? But thanks be to God that though you were slaves of sin, you became obedient from the heart to that form of teaching to which you were committed, and having been freed from sin, you became slaves of righteousness.

First the apostle Paul states the obvious fact that when someone presents himself as the slave of someone else, the primary issue is obedience—doing what the master says. That is true whether someone is an unbeliever and a servant to sin, or a believer and a servant to Christ.

Paul then takes that simple illustration and applies it to the crucial phrase "obedient from the heart" in verse 17. Heart obedience ought to be an overriding attitude and desire for any Christian. He or she ought to have such a strong desire for obedience that he or she constantly manifests obedience as a fundamental, inner trait of his or her Christian life. Believers become so obedient to what God's Word teaches them that they become "slaves of righteousness" (v. 18).

Other New Testament passages make it clear that it's not enough for believers simply to hear or read the Word (see Jesus' stern warning and sobering illustration in Matthew 7:21-27). The essential question is, Are they obeying it?

The apostle James addresses the importance of obedience when he declares, "Prove yourselves doers of the word, and not merely hearers who delude themselves" (1:22). Whenever someone is not regularly applying Scripture to his life, he is deceived about his true spiritual condition. James illustrates this principle this way: "For if anyone is a hearer of the word and not a doer, he is like a man who looks [literally, glances] at his natural face in a mirror; for once he has looked at himself and gone away, he has immediately forgotten what kind of person he was" (vv. 23-24). Let me illustrate this further with a more contemporary example.

Suppose a man decides one day to shave off his beard or mustache. While he's shaving, he's interrupted by a phone call. When he completes his conversation, he forgets that he had been shaving and instead finishes dressing and goes to work, only to encounter the hilarious greetings of his coworkers, who tell him how silly he looks. That's what it's like with anyone who merely glances at the Word, turns away, and does not apply it. He doesn't realize how bad his spiritual condition is and is deceived about his true spiritual needs.

That certainly applies to an unbeliever who hears the Gospel but does not take time to seriously consider it. The words of truth don't penetrate, and he remains deceived about his true condition. James 1:23-24 can also apply to a person who comes to church, hears the Word preached, makes a profession of faith, thinks he's a Christian, but never applies anything he hears.

Regrettably, a genuine believer can also be deceived about the spiritual improvement he needs to make. He hears teaching about a certain area of the Christian life in which he falls sinfully short. But instead of applying Scripture to the deficient area, he lives as he did before and is deceived about the true status of his spiritual life.

James concludes by presenting a profile of the obedient Christian: "But one who looks intently at the perfect law, the law of liberty, and abides by it, not having become a forgetful hearer but an effectual doer, this man shall be blessed in what he does" (v. 25). In the original Greek, the verb "looks intently" refers to taking a close, prolonged look in order to properly assess something. You are to examine the perfect law of liberty, which is God's Word that sets you free from sin and death (cf. John 8:32; 1 Pet. 1:23-25; 2:2), and abide by it. Only by being "an effectual doer" rather than "a forgetful hearer" will you be ultimately blessed. An attitude of obedience brings true blessing.

In conclusion, when we experienced salvation, we also made a simple but far-reaching covenant of obedience with the Lord. Therefore, the attitude of obedience must accompany the attitude of faith in the Christian life because they are both critical to our salvation. Those churches blessed to have believers exhibiting the twin pillars of faith and obedience will also be filled with joy, power, and blessings from God.

3

BLESSED ARE THE HUMBLE

True spirituality, which is always characterized by biblical faith and obedience, is also accompanied by the attitude of humility. This attitude is at the very center of the Christian life. It is the foundation of all graces, and yet so much of what passes for Christianity these days emphasizes pride and self-esteem, which were also prominent in the Judaism of Jesus' day. The Jews, notably the scribes and Pharisees, paraded their external religion before others and expected to receive flattering praise in return. Jesus exposed that hypocrisy when He taught the twelve and other disciples the following:

> They [the religious leaders] do all their deeds to be noticed by men; for they broaden their phylacteries, and lengthen the tassels of their garments. And they love the place of honor at banquets, and the chief seats in the synagogues, and respectful greetings in the market places, and being called by men, Rabbi. But do not be called Rabbi; for One is your Teacher, and you are all brothers. And do not call anyone on earth your father; for One is your Father, He who is in heaven. And do not be called leaders; for One is your Leader, that is, Christ. But the greatest among you shall be your servant. And whoever exalts himself shall be humbled; and whoever humbles himself shall be exalted.
>
> —Matt. 23:5-12

JESUS' TEACHING ON HUMILITY

The Jewish leaders obviously had not heeded the Lord's earlier instruction against spiritual pride, which He took aim at in the opening sentences of the Beatitudes: "Blessed are the poor in spirit, for theirs is the kingdom of heaven. Blessed are those who mourn, for they shall be comforted. Blessed are the gentle, for they shall inherit the earth. Blessed are those who hunger and thirst for righteousness, for they shall be satisfied" (Matt. 5:3-6). Each of those godly attitudes, with its accompanying promise, describes people who are in the kingdom of God. They identify those people who have comfort in all the important issues of life and who can look forward to someday inheriting the earth in its ultimate form—the glories of the new heaven and the new earth. And each Beatitude is descriptive of a facet of humility.

Poverty of Spirit

Christ begins the Sermon with the phrase, "Blessed are the poor in spirit." "Poor" is from the Greek *ptochos*, which means one who is so poor he has to beg. It was used specifically of beggars who had no work skill or were too disabled to work. Such poor people were financially bankrupt, utterly destitute, and without any means of support.

The kingdom of God belongs to the spiritually destitute. All who are genuinely saved have realized their own spiritual bankruptcy; thus they knew they could not enter based on any worth of their own. In the final analysis, the kingdom belongs to everyone who has been, like the tax collector in Jesus' parable, "even unwilling to lift up his eyes to heaven, but was beating his breast, saying, 'God, be merciful to me, the sinner!'" (Luke 18:13).

By contrast, membership in the kingdom of God does not belong to those who are counting on their baptism, their church upbringing, or their Christian heritage. Kingdom membership also does not belong to people who are counting solely on some date when they "made a decision for Christ" or went forward at the end of a service. Likewise, those who take pride in conformity to all the external forms of their church tradition, who give regularly to various ministries, and who are always busy with religious activities cannot presume to have automatic membership in the kingdom. The only ones who can claim such assurance are those who have humbly cast themselves on God's mercy, were cleansed of their sins, and therefore "went down to [their] house justified," as Jesus described the tax collector in Luke 18:14.

Spiritual Mourning

People who understand and are dealing with their spiritual bankruptcy also "mourn" over their sin. This is not the improper mourning that displays sorrow over sinful plans that are frustrated (see 2 Sam. 13:2) or that manifests a prolonged, depressed sorrow or an abnormal amount of grief due to misguided loyalties and affections (see 2 Sam. 18:33—19:6). That kind of mourning is wrong and often is related to selfish guilt, unfaithfulness, and a sinful lack of trust in the Lord.

The mourning Jesus speaks of in Matthew 5:4 is not even the same as the legitimate kind, which we all display from time to time as a normal part of life, such as when a loved one dies (see Gen. 23:2). Neither is it the kind of mourning that believers do when they are discouraged in ministry (2 Tim. 1:3-4), when they are grieved over another's sins (Jer. 9:1), when they are concerned for the spiritual welfare of other Christians (Acts 20:31, 37-38), or when they are distressed about the difficulties of a relative or friend (Mark 9:24).

Jesus truly knows about all those rightful sorrows of believers, and He will provide them all the help they need to cope with trials; but that is not the issue in Matthew 5. In verse 4 He is referring to a godly mourning that only those who are earnestly seeking Him for salvation or those who already know Him can experience. Paul commended the Corinthians for such godly mourning (sorrow): "For the sorrow that is according to the will of God produces a repentance without regret, leading to salvation; but the sorrow of the world produces death. For behold what earnestness this very thing, this godly sorrow, has produced in you" (2 Cor. 7:10-11).

Of the nine different Greek terms used in the New Testament

for *sorrow*, the one translated "mourn" in Matthew 5:4 and elsewhere represents the strongest feelings and the most heartfelt grief (cf. Mark 16:10; Rev. 18:11, 15; and Gen. 37:34 [Greek Old Testament]). It further conveys the concept of deep inward agony, sometimes accompanied by outward weeping and wailing. When David mourned over his sin and confessed it, he declared, "How blessed is he whose transgression is forgiven, whose sin is covered! How blessed is the man to whom the LORD does not impute iniquity, and in whose spirit there is no deceit!" (Ps. 32:1-2).

In Matthew 5:4, Jesus uses the present participle *penthountes*, indicating continuous action. Faithful and mature believers will have a constant, lifelong attitude of mourning or brokenness over sin, which will allow them to see more and more of God's love and mercy and less and less of their own pride. The true expression of this attitude (it will not wallow in self-pity or false humility) does not focus on the person and his or her sin, but humbly and happily looks to God, who alone can forgive iniquity. It is the attitude Paul expressed in Romans 7 as he described his ongoing battle with sin, which he concluded by saying, "Wretched man that I am! Who will set me free from the body of this death? Thanks be to God through Jesus Christ our Lord!" (vv. 24-25).

If we continually mourn over sin, we will be continually comforted. Although we can know this comfort in the present (Matt. 11:28; 2 Thess. 2:16), it will be complete only in the glory of heaven, where God "shall wipe away every tear from their eyes; and there shall no longer be any death; there shall no longer be any mourning, or crying, or pain" (Rev. 21:4).

Gentleness

The attitude of gentleness (Matt. 5:5), according to our Lord's divine wisdom, fits next in the way He logically presents the Beatitudes. Poverty of spirit leads us to turn away from our sinful selves and mourn because of our unrighteousness. Then gentleness, which is also a product of our humility, will cause us to seek God's righteousness.

The Greek word (*praos*), rendered "gentle" in verse 5, essentially means "mild" or "soft" and sometimes described a soothing medicine or a soft breeze. It also described the temperament of animals whose naturally wild spirits had been broken to make them useful as work animals. In humans it defined an attitude that was meek, submissive, quiet, and tenderhearted. Though Jesus, during His triumphal entry into Jerusalem, was hailed as the King of the Jews, Matthew also says He was "gentle, and mounted upon a donkey" (21:5).

Gentleness has always been God's will for His people. Job 5:11 says that God "sets on high those who are lowly, and those who mourn are lifted to safety." Moses is described as being "very humble, more than any man who was on the face of the earth" (Num. 12:3). And David, the man after God's own heart, wrote, "He [the Lord] leads the humble in justice, and He teaches the humble His way" (Ps. 25:9).

Gentleness is also stressed throughout the New Testament. In addition to Jesus' teaching on it, Paul had much to say. The apostle urged the Ephesian believers to "walk in a manner worthy of the calling with which you have been called, with all humility and gentleness, with patience, showing forbearance to one another in love" (Eph. 4:1-2). He instructed Titus to remind his people "to be subject to rulers, to authorities, to be obedient, to be ready for every good deed, to malign no one, to be uncontentious, gentle, showing every consideration for all men" (Titus 3:1-2).

In English, the word *gentleness* (and especially its older synonym *meekness*) may often connote weakness, but that is a misunderstanding of the scriptural meaning. Gentleness is power placed under control, as the writer of Proverbs says: "He who is slow to anger is better than the mighty, and he who rules his spirit, than he who captures a city" (16:32). In contrast, the individual who is not gentle is likened to "a city that is broken into and without walls" (Prov. 25:28). Gentleness always uses its resources appropriately, unlike the out-of-control emotions that so often are destructive and have no place in the life of the believer.

Gentleness also should not be equated with cowardice, lack of conviction, or mere human niceness. Instead, it is a virtue that draws courage, strength, conviction, and a good disposition from God, not from self-centered human resources. Gentleness was characteristic of our Lord Jesus Christ, who always defended God's glory and ultimately gave Himself in sacrifice for others (see 1 Pet. 2:21-24). Although He did not lash back when criticized, slandered, or treated unjustly, Jesus responded fittingly and firmly when God's honor was profaned or His truth was perverted or neglected. He twice cleansed the Temple by force (John 2:14-16; Matt. 21:12-17), and He repeatedly and fearlessly denounced the hypocrisy of the Jewish religious leaders (Matt. 23:13-36; Mark 12:13-40; John 8:12-59; 9:39-41).

Like Christ, the gentle person does not defend himself. That's because he has died to self and therefore does not worry about insult, material loss, or even personal injury. The believer who has gentleness knows that in himself he does not deserve defending and that in the long run all his possessions are not worth fighting for. In that sense, gentleness is the opposite of violence and vengeance.

The result of gentleness, according to Jesus, is that those who have it "shall inherit the earth" (Matt. 5:5). God will someday reclaim His earthly domain, which was marred by the Fall, and believers will rule that domain with Him. Therefore those who are gentle—all true Christians—can trust completely in Jesus' promise. Our Lord's use of the emphatic Greek pronoun *autos* indicates that *only* the gentle will inherit the earth with Him.

The Greek term for "inherit" (*kleronomeō*) means "to receive one's allotted portion or rightful inheritance." It is a promise, along with Psalm 37:11, that in spite of the present prosperity of many unbelievers and the suffering that many believers now endure, a time of reckoning is coming. The unbeliever (unless he repents and believes) will be judged, and the believer will inherit the blessing God has promised.

The meting out of judgment and the granting of blessing is in God's sovereign hands and will be accomplished precisely in His time and according to His will. In the meantime, His children are to live in faith and obedience, with gentleness, knowing that then they "shall inherit the earth."

Spiritual Hunger and Thirst

The fourth Beatitude—"Blessed are those who hunger and thirst for righteousness, for they shall be satisfied" (Matt. 5:6)—is more positive and flows from the previous three. When someone dies to himself, mourns over his sinfulness, and turns over his power to God's control, he will receive a strong desire for righteousness and an intense longing for more of what God has.

Martyn Lloyd-Jones defines the importance of Matthew 5:6:

This Beatitude . . . is a statement to which all the others lead. It is the logical conclusion to which they come, and it is something for which we should all be profoundly thankful and grateful to God. I do not know of a better test that anyone can apply to himself or herself in this whole matter of the Christian profession than a verse like this. If this verse is to you one of the most blessed statements of the whole Scripture, you can be quite certain you are a Christian. If it is not, then you had better examine the foundations again. (*Studies in the Sermon on the Mount* [Grand Rapids, Mich.: Eerdmans, 1971], 1:73-74)

Even though genuine believers still struggle with unredeemed flesh (cf. Rom. 8:23), they desire to know and obey more and more of God's truth. This is evident from David's confession: "O how I love Thy law" (Ps. 119:97). The apostle Paul testifies to the same passion for righteousness: "I joyfully concur with the law of God in the inner man" (Rom. 7:22).

The following true story from World War I is an excellent illustration of the intense meaning Jesus' phrase "hunger and thirst" conveys. When Palestine was liberated, a combined force of troops from the British Empire closely pursued the retreating Turks across the desert. The Allied soldiers soon outdistanced their water-carrying camel train as they passed Beersheba and pushed northward. Before long the men ran out of water and began feeling the ill effects. Their mouths dried up, and their lips swelled and became purple. They suffered headaches, dizziness, and faintness. Their bloodshot and bleary eyes saw mirages. In desperation they all realized they had to reach the wells at Sheriah by nightfall to avoid suffering thousands of fatalities. Hundreds had already died of thirst; so the others fought hard and drove the Turkish forces from Sheriah.

After the battle, the strongest British troops were required to stand at attention near the giant stone cisterns as water was distributed to the wounded and those about to go on guard duty. While the needy refreshed themselves, the other men were not more than twenty feet from thousands of gallons of water. They had agonized for many days to reach all that fresh water, and yet they were forced to wait an additional four hours before enjoying it.

One of the officers who witnessed that march reportedly made this spiritual application: "I believe that we all learned our first real Bible lesson on the march from Beersheba to Sheriah Wells. If such were our thirst for God, for righteousness and for His will in our lives, a consuming, all-embracing, preoccupying desire, how rich in the fruit of the Spirit would we be?" (E.M. Blaiklock, "Water," *Eternity* [August 1966], 27).

That illustration shows that Jesus used the most powerful natural impulses and longings to represent how we as believers should deeply desire righteousness. "Hunger" and "thirst" are both present participles, signifying a continuous longing and seeking. If we know Christ, we will continually yearn after holiness, just as we longed to know Him at our salvation. Sinlessness and complete likeness to the Lord do not occur until we reach heaven; therefore, we always need to be, and should never stop, hungering for greater and greater growth in sanctification. This is an attitude we will have every day (cf. Luke 6:21) if we are truly humble. Paul prayed that the Philippians' "love may abound still more and more in real knowledge and all discernment, so that you may approve the things that are excellent, in order to be sincere and blameless until the day of Christ" (Phil. 1:9-10).

Another feature of spiritual hunger is that its object is all-encompassing. That is clearly seen in the grammar of Matthew 5:6. Jesus uses the Greek accusative genitive for "righteousness," which makes it the unqualified, complete object of "hunger and thirst." Those who truly long for righteousness will be longing for all the righteousness there is (cf. 5:48; 1 Pet. 1:15-16).

Our Lord also uses the Greek definite article (not included in most English translations) before "righteousness," which denotes a special kind of righteousness—*the* righteousness—that which is true and comes only from God, because it actually resides in Him.

Finally, the attitude of spiritual hunger is unconditional. If we have such hunger, we will seek and accept God's righteousness no matter how He provides it, and we will obey His commands no matter how challenging or difficult they may be. We will not be like the rich young ruler (Mark 10:17-22) who hungered for worldly things more than for the things of God. His self-centered conditions for God's blessings prevented him from receiving them. The spiritually hungry want only Christ and His kingdom (cf. Ps. 119:20; Isa. 26:9)—even if that means not having some of the material riches that people in the world have.

The attitudes Jesus taught in Matthew 5:3-6 are to characterize believers throughout their entire earthly lives. If you're a Christian, you don't become more worthy of salvation or more worthy of God's goodness than when you first entered the kingdom. You still sin, and it is still God's grace that sustains you. Therefore, there is never a time or a place for selfish pride to be exercised in your life. Whatever godly traits and noble works may be manifest in you are the work of the Lord, not of your own ingenuity or innate goodness. That's why Peter exhorts us in 1 Peter 5:5-6, "All of you, clothe yourselves with humility toward one another, for God is opposed to the proud, but gives grace to the humble. Humble yourselves, therefore, under the mighty hand of God, that He may exalt you at the proper time."

PAUL'S THORN IN THE FLESH

There is no doubt that God wants believers to have humility. But because of their remaining sinfulness, God sometimes does whatever is necessary to humble them. Even the apostle Paul experienced

God's humbling work in the midst of his ministry, not just at his conversion on the Damascus road:

> *I will go on to visions and revelations of the Lord. I know a man in Christ who fourteen years ago—whether in the body I do not know, or out of the body I do not know, God knows—such a man was caught up to the third heaven. And I know how such a man—whether in the body or apart from the body I do not know, God knows—was caught up into Paradise, and heard inexpressible words, which a man is not permitted to speak. On behalf of such a man will I boast; but on my own behalf I will not boast, except in regard to my weaknesses. For if I do wish to boast I shall not be foolish, for I shall be speaking the truth; but I refrain from this, so that no one may credit me with more than he sees in me or hears from me. And because of the surpassing greatness of the revelations, for this reason, to keep me from exalting myself, there was given me a thorn in the flesh, a messenger of Satan to buffet me— to keep me from exalting myself! Concerning this I entreated the Lord three times that it might depart from me. And He has said to me, "My grace is sufficient for you, for power is perfected in weakness." Most gladly, therefore, I will rather boast about my weaknesses, that the power of Christ may dwell in me.*
> *—2 Cor. 12:1-9*

Even though he speaks rather obliquely in verse 2 of "a man in Christ," the context makes it obvious that Paul is referring to himself. He mentions an extraordinary, supernatural experience he had fourteen years earlier (probably sometime between his return to Tarsus from Jerusalem [Acts 9:30] and the beginning of His missionary journeys [Acts 13:1-3]), the details and reality of which he did not understand and could not fully explain. He was not sure if he was taken to heaven bodily, or if his spirit was somehow temporarily translated out of his body. But God knows how it happened, and that's what matters.

Whatever the details, Paul was wondrously transported to "the third heaven" (the same place as "Paradise"), the abode of God

Almighty and the place of His throne. Despite incomplete and imprecise understanding concerning how things happened, Paul repeated, as if for emphasis, his assertion that he truly had been taken to heaven. He was certain the event did occur, and he even heard words of supernatural origin, spoken to him alone. So this experience was unique to Paul, no matter what many charismatics or mystics may claim today. The words he heard were also special—"inexpressible words, which a man is not permitted to speak" (v. 4), and beyond what the text says, we cannot know what they were.

But the various unknowns of Paul's account are beside the point. His real purpose in writing about his incredible experience is to relate what he learned about humility. The apostle knew he had not been granted a special trip to heaven because he was so spiritual and deserved the privilege. Although a part of him wanted to celebrate and rejoice at the memory of such a journey, he was more inclined to look back and rejoice in his weakness.

This incident and several other visions and revelations (e.g., Acts 9:3-18; 16:9-10; 27:23-24; Gal. 1:12; 2:2; Eph. 3:3) could easily have caused the apostle to be elevated with pride and feelings of superiority. That's why 2 Corinthians 12:7 says, "For this reason, to keep me from exalting myself, there was given me a thorn in the flesh, a messenger of Satan to buffet me—to keep me from exalting myself."

Paul writes metaphorically of a "thorn," but the agent of his humility is better likened to a sharp stake that could be driven right through his otherwise proud flesh. It was not some small thing like a thorn on a rosebush, but something significant enough to truly humble him. In fact, it was a messenger from Satan whom God allowed to keep Paul from being puffed up with pride. And it's clear this person was allowed by God to afflict Paul because the apostle to no avail asked the Lord three times to remove the thorn.

I believe this particular reference to a demon-possessed or satanically inspired person was to the ringleader of the Corinthian false teachers who were conspiring against Paul and devouring the church at Corinth. Undoubtedly, Paul did not like being backed against the wall by his opponents at Corinth and quite likely prayed that God would destroy them, even as David prayed in the imprecatory psalms regarding his enemies. But God wanted to use the leader of Paul's foes as an instrument to humble him. The Lord was willing, as He often is, to use whatever extremity necessary to humble one of His servants, even if it meant sending a messenger from Satan to plague Paul, allowing divisions in the Corinthian church to challenge him, or permitting his enemies at Corinth to directly test him by maligning his character. To God it is crucial that believers understand and embrace the attitude of humility.

Second Corinthians 12:9 further explains just how important humility is for us who know Christ: "And He has said to me, 'My grace is sufficient for you, for power is perfected in weakness.' Most gladly, therefore, I will rather boast about my weaknesses, that the power of Christ may dwell in me." God leveled Paul and taught him that when he was at the end of himself and had nothing, then he was most usable in ministry. The apostle thus came to realize that spiritual power is directly related to humility and brokenness. He searched his heart, let the Lord's humbling work go forward, and learned to embrace adversity—false accusations, malicious criticisms and character attacks, and much misrepresentation of his motives. Those are the same things we often must do if we would display a genuine attitude of humility.

THE MARKS OF THE HUMBLE PERSON

Some of the truest marks of the humble Christian are summarized in Paul's exhortation to the Philippians: "Do nothing from selfishness or empty conceit, but with humility of mind let each of you regard one another as more important than himself; do not merely look out for your own personal interests, but also for the interests of others" (2:3-4).

The first basic mark of the humble person is that he sees his own sin as worse than others'. Paul himself was a perfect example of this attitude: "Christ Jesus came into the world to save sinners, among whom I am foremost of all" (1 Tim. 1:15). When it's *our* sins that most grieve and offend us and are the ones we most want to avoid, then we demonstrate a real measure of humility.

A second mark of the humble person is that he or she is not self-centered (Phil. 2:4). Selfless people are more concerned with the lives of others, including their enterprises, their successes and failures, their blessings and disappointments, and their prosperity or poverty. Their own interests, privileges, popularity, achievements, or reputations are secondary when compared to the needs of others.

Of course, the Lord Jesus had the supreme attitude of selflessness, as expressed in Philippians 2:5-8:

> *Have this attitude in yourselves which was also in Christ Jesus, who, although He existed in the form of God, did not regard equality with God a thing to be grasped, but emptied Himself, taking the form of a bond-servant, and being made in the likeness of men. And being found in appearance as a man, He humbled Himself by becoming obedient to the point of death, even death on a cross.*

Christ was perfectly willing to set aside His divine privileges and be separated from the Father to endure inexplicable, incomprehensible agony so that we might be saved. This marvelous and familiar passage underscores the magnitude of our Lord and Savior's humility on our behalf. He condescended to our human level—even taking on the role of a bond-servant—so that in His sacrificial death He could fulfill God's plan of redemption for all of us who have faith and obedience in Him.

The attitude of humility comes full circle—back to Jesus Christ and what He humbly did for spiritually bankrupt, completely unworthy sinners. That brings us back to what our attitude must be if we would reap the benefits of His atoning work and enter His kingdom. It's the attitude Jesus urged the disciples to have:

> *At that time the disciples came to Jesus, saying, "Who then is greatest in the kingdom of heaven?" And He called a child to Himself and set him in their midst, and said, "Truly I say to you, unless*

you are converted and become like children, you shall not enter the kingdom of heaven. Whoever then humbles himself as this child, he is the greatest in the kingdom of heaven."

—*Matt. 18:1-4*

Right in the midst of the disciples' prideful debate among themselves about who would be greatest in the kingdom, Jesus used a little child to illustrate humility. A child is totally dependent, and that's the attitude we must bring as we seek entrance into God's kingdom. We must enter with childlike faith and obedience, and we must live every day of the Christian life with an attitude of childlike humility. As Augustus Toplady wrote in the third stanza of his great hymn "Rock of Ages":

> *Nothing in my hand I bring,*
> *Simply to thy cross I cling;*
> *Naked, come to thee for dress,*
> *Helpless, look to thee for grace.*

4

THE SELFLESS NATURE OF LOVE

J. C. Ryle, the nineteenth-century evangelical Anglican bishop, wrote the following about love in 1878:

> Charity [love] is rightly called "the Queen of Christian graces." "The end of the commandment," says St. Paul, "is charity." (1 Tim. i.5.) It is a grace which all people profess to admire. It seems a plain practical thing which everybody can understand. It is none of "those troublesome doctrinal points" about which Christians are disagreed. Thousands, I suspect, would not be ashamed to tell you that they knew nothing about justification or regeneration, about the work of Christ or the Holy Spirit. But nobody, I believe, would like to say that he knew nothing about "charity!" If men possess nothing else in religion, they always flatter themselves that they possess "charity." (*Practical Religion* [1878; Grand Rapids, Mich.: Baker Books, 1977], 165)

Unfortunately, not much has changed in more than 100 years. The concept of love is still misunderstood, distorted, and wrongly defined by the average person, thanks largely to our media and entertainment-dominated popular culture. Love is defined in subjective and sensual terms in countless popular songs of the past several generations. It is trivialized constantly in the daily stream of commercials and advertisements that confront us through television, radio, news-papers, magazines, and now the Internet. And many Christians are confused by the contemporary emphasis on "love and toleration" that promotes an ecumenical blurring of doctrinal distinctives (e.g., between evangelicals and Catholics), all in the name of "cooperative ministry" to advance certain social, family, and moral agendas that will supposedly improve the culture.

LOVE BIBLICALLY DEFINED

As it is for any sinful, erroneous, or muddled perspective on a spiritual topic, the Bible is the best source for clarifying our thinking about love. God's Word makes numerous references to love, but Ephesians 5:1-2 provides us with an entry point for the subject and an excellent definition of love: "Therefore be imitators of God, as beloved children; and walk in love, just as Christ also loved you, and gave Himself up for us, an offering and a sacrifice to God as a fragrant aroma."

If you want to imitate God and be known as His child, walk in love because God Himself is love (1 John 4:8; cf. John 3:16). The Greek word for "imitators" (*mimētēs*) is the root of our English word *mimic*, one who copies another individual's specific characteristics. As believers, we are to imitate God's traits, which would definitely include His love. His purpose in salvation was to redeem us from sin and to conform us "to the image of His Son" (Rom. 8:29). Peter commands us, "Do not be conformed to the former lusts which were yours in your ignorance, but like the Holy One who called you, be holy yourselves also in all your behavior; because it is written, 'You shall be holy, for I am holy'" (1 Pet. 1:14-16; cf. Lev. 11:44).

We can imitate God only as we let Christ live His perfect life through us and depend completely on His indwelling Spirit (Rom. 5:5; Eph. 3:16, 19). Then we will be able to "let all that you do be done in love" (1 Cor. 16:14).

Just as children instinctively imitate their parents' actions and behaviors, spiritual children should want to imitate God because He has given them the right to be His children (John 1:12; Gal. 3:26). For all of us who are believers, that was His plan from eternity past: God "predestined us to adoption as sons through Jesus Christ to Himself, according to the kind intention of His will" (Eph. 1:5). So, as children of God it becomes natural for us to be as He is in every respect—holy, kind, forgiving, humble, and loving.

The noblest divine characteristic we can imitate is sacrificial love. As Ephesians 5:2 says, Jesus "gave Himself up for us." That was the height of *agapē* love—not simply good feelings about someone else, but unconditionally giving oneself for the welfare of another (cf. 1 John 3:16). Christ did not sacrifice Himself for us because we were so deserving (Rom. 5:8, 10), but purely from His sovereign, gracious love, paying sin's enormous penalty for all who believe.

The difference is evident between God's unconditional love and conditional human love. Conditional love is manifested when people withhold their love from anyone who doesn't fulfill their expectations. That often occurs between a husband and wife. That kind of love ebbs and flows and sometimes disappears from the marriage, which can result in separation or divorce. But loss of romantic love is not a scriptural reason to dissolve a marriage, because God commands husbands to love their wives unconditionally, just as He loves us (Eph. 5:25; Titus 2:4). Romantic love certainly improves the marriage relationship, but the love that ultimately holds a Christian marriage together is God's type of love, which continues to give even when it doesn't receive.

Ephesians 5:2 is the clearest, most precise definition of the attitude of love found anywhere in God's Word. Love is not primarily an emotion that makes us feel warm and sentimental. Rather, it is an act of self-sacrifice. We realize that when we see that God loved us, as evidenced by the sacrifice His Son made for us. An attitude of genuine love will give magnanimously, over and over, and will go to the greatest lengths imaginable, all with no concern for itself.

THE WORLD'S PERVERSION OF LOVE

As I said at the beginning of this chapter, the world for the most part knows nothing about the biblical definition of love. The apostle Paul highlights this fact by contrasting the believer's need to copy God's love (Eph. 5:1-2) and to avoid the world's perverse expressions of love: "But do not let immorality or any impurity or greed even be named among you, as is proper among saints" (5:3).

Satan always counterfeits the good things God establishes. In contrast to God's unconditional, unselfish love, Satan promotes a lustful and self-indulgent love. The objects of worldly love are only those who are somehow attractive, enjoyable, satisfying, and reciprocal. Such love can be reciprocal, but it gives little and expects to get much in return. Our Lord had no praise for this distorted kind of love: "For if you love those who love you, what reward have you? Do not even the tax-gatherers do the same?" (Matt. 5:46).

It's no surprise that Satan's brand of love inevitably leads to immorality and impurity. Today if someone is single and "falls in love," it often leads to fornication. If someone is married and "falls in love" with a person other than his or her spouse, that often leads to an adulterous affair. If someone "falls in love" with another person of the same sex, that person assumes it's all right to engage in homosexual activity.

The Greek term in Ephesians 5:3 that encompasses the various forms of sexual sin ("immorality") is *porneia*, from which we get the English word *pornography*. It is the opposite of the Greek *enkrateia*, which usually referred to sexual self-control. That is the term Luke used in Acts 24:25 to describe Paul's confrontation of the governor Felix—"discussing righteousness, *self-control* and the judgment to come" (emphasis added). The apostle in essence told Felix, who had stolen his wife Drusilla from her former husband and was therefore committing adultery, that he was sinning by refusing to discipline his sexual desire, and he was therefore under God's judgment.

Loss of sexual self-control also leads to "impurity" (*akatharsia*), a more inclusive term than *porneia*. Jesus used *akatharsia* to describe the rottenness in tombs (Matt. 23:27), but its other New Testament usages refer to lustful passions, impure ideas, fantasies, and all other forms of sexual sin.

Immorality and impurity are both expressions of selfish sexual "greed," and greed in general is contrary to the self-giving nature of love. This kind of greed disguises itself as something attractive and rewarding, but in reality it is harmful and hateful because it does not unselfishly seek the purity of others, as love does. Because sexual greed can seem so good and can have such a powerful appeal, spouses forsake each other, families neglect or destroy each other, and friends hate each other.

Strong sexual greed will often stop at nothing on its way to fulfilling its lusts. Because such powerful urges exist within people, sexual sin has gotten totally out of control, accompanied by complete insensitivity to others' feelings and well-being, terrible violence and savagery, and even murder. Sadly, one phenomenon of the past generation that has produced barbaric consequences is legalized abortion.

Proponents and practitioners of abortion, and those many women who have actually undergone the procedure, are all examples of how steeped in self-love western culture is and how far it has gone in applying sexually sinful definitions to personal relationships. The abortion battle is not over the right merely to kill babies—only the most outwardly sadistic individuals would advocate that. The underlying reason people want to have the option of abortion is to maintain their "sexual freedom" and personal convenience. Their demand for such "rights" is so overwhelming that their solution to the unwanted consequences of sexual relations is not to stop the promiscuity, but to kill the unborn children that result. People are so obsessed with being able to have sex without implications or responsibilities that they're willing to rationalize the murder of society's most defenseless and innocent members. As one contemporary writer has bluntly stated it, "Abortion is the willingness to kill for the sake of the willingness to copulate."

FALSE LOVE'S CORRUPTION OF THE CULTURE

Western society has such an obsessive focus and preoccupation on sexual pleasure that it has corrupted the culture to the core. This corruption is a primary product of the massive culture war that is raging today. Believers do not always realize the extent, nature, or intensity of the conflict, but it goes back many centuries to what Augustine called the battle between the city of God and the city of man. He saw an ongoing struggle between biblical Christianity and the satanic world system. Within our culture's moral realm, the conflict is almost exclusively about sex—heterosexual and homosexual promiscuity, divorce, abortion, and feminism. All of these make outright assaults against genuine love.

In the culture war being waged against God's kingdom, Satan seems to be using a six-step plan to rally the forces of his worldly kingdom. We can envision his plan unfolding somewhat along these lines:

(1) Satan's ultimate goal is to win souls to his cause.

(2) A powerful and effective way Satan gains adherents to his system is to corrupt society. He simply makes his own corollary out of the maxim that a good society is one that makes it easier for people to be good, and a bad society is one that makes it easier for people to be bad. Satan influences society toward evil by exploiting people's tendencies to conform to the opinions, ideologies, and trends set forth by the news, advertising, and entertainment media. He accomplishes that by simply manipulating those culturally influential forces of communication. Daily we see examples of the devil's controlling the media (the excessively worldly quality of network television programming, the disproportionately large amount of secular bias in news reporting, sexually and violently graphic movies, a saturation of materialistic and hedonistic advertising, and so on). Satan's success rate can be measured by how much easier it is to be bad as society grows worse and worse.

(3) Another powerful means Satan uses to corrupt society is his destruction of the family, a fundamental cultural building block where sacrificial love can be learned on a daily basis.

(4) He can ruin the family by destroying marriage.

(5) He can destroy marriage by weakening sexual fidelity, the glue that bonds it together.

(6) Finally, Satan destroys sexual fidelity by means of the sexual revolution. This revolution, which got jump-started in the 1960s, demands that people be free to do whatever they want sexually. As we

have seen, it is the centerpiece of the tragic redefinition and distortion of the biblical ideal of love. It is also the devil's most strategic tool in waging the culture war against the city of God and all who trust in Him.

The sexual revolution will perhaps prove to be the most destructive revolution in history, far worse than any political or military revolution we've known. While western culture was preoccupied with the Cold War and worried about the Soviet Union and its satellite nations behind the Iron Curtain, the nuclear arms race, the space race, threats of foreign espionage, and many other external menaces, the sexual revolution was steadily eroding and destroying the very foundations of society. It is the prevailing cultural force that has led us to our current state of corruption and moral relativism.

Modern society is a picture of a culture that has completely redefined love—away from one's self-sacrificial and unconditional concern for others' welfare to one's greedy, lustful concern for sexual freedom and "fulfillment." Nothing could be further from a proper scriptural understanding of love. However, the new definition does bear out what Ephesians 5:3-7 warns us about. But the question remains: How will today's selfish, sex-saturated society ever see genuine love displayed? The answer is profoundly illustrated by our Lord in John 13.

CHRIST'S PRACTICAL EXAMPLE OF LOVE

John 13 provides us with a penetrating insight into the desperately needed, divinely inspired attitude of love. The apostle John recounts Jesus' practical demonstration:

> *Now before the Feast of the Passover, Jesus knowing that His hour had come that He should depart out of this world to the Father, having loved His own who were in the world, He loved them to the end. And during supper, the devil having already put into the heart of Judas Iscariot, the son of Simon, to betray Him, Jesus, knowing that the Father had given all things into His hands, and that He had come forth from God, and was going back to God, rose from supper, and laid aside His garments; and taking a towel, girded Himself*

about. Then He poured water into the basin, and began to wash the disciples' feet, and to wipe them with the towel with which He was girded. And so He came to Simon Peter. He said to Him, "Lord, do You wash my feet?" Jesus answered and said to him, "What I do you do not realize now; but you shall understand hereafter." Peter said to Him, "Never shall You wash my feet!" Jesus answered him, "If I do not wash you, you have no part with Me." Simon Peter said to Him, "Lord, not my feet only, but also my hands and my head." Jesus said to him, "He who has bathed needs only to wash his feet, but is completely clean; and you are clean, but not all of you." For He knew the one who was betraying Him; for this reason He said, "Not all of you are clean." And so when He had washed their feet, and taken His garments, and reclined at the table again, He said to them, "Do you know what I have done to you? You call Me Teacher and Lord; and you are right, for so I am. If I then, the Lord and the Teacher, washed your feet, you also ought to wash one another's feet. For I gave you an example that you also should do as I did to you. Truly, truly, I say to you, a slave is not greater than his master; neither is one who is sent greater than the one who sent him. If you know these things, you are blessed if you do them."

—13:1-17

This episode took place, of course, in the Upper Room, during that fateful evening before Jesus was crucified and when Judas Iscariot treacherously betrayed Him to the Jewish religious leaders and the Roman authorities. Meanwhile, the other disciples had been caught up in a selfish debate about which of them would be greatest in the kingdom of God. None of them seemed to have the least bit of sensitivity or consideration for what the Lord was about to endure, even though just recently He had told them He would soon die and not be with them much longer. All those negative factors would have made the disciples most unlovable by normal human standards, but verse 1 says the Son of God "loved His own who were in the world, [and] He loved them to the end." Christ's love toward His own was (and is) unconditional. He loved the disciples to the utmost, even when they displayed the ugliest indifference to Him.

Verse 3 begins to unfold the actual demonstration of Jesus' love. He knew God the Father had sovereignly given all things into His hands, that He had been sent to earth by the Father, and that He would return to God at the proper time. There is no question that Jesus agonized (in the Garden of Gethsemane) over the coming reality of His substitutionary death on the cross, but He had no fear regarding the outcome of events (cf. John 17).

With the perfect assurance that all the surrounding events were under God's control, Jesus turned His loving attention toward the disciples (v. 4). He took off His outer garment and stripped down to His undergarments, probably leaving His legs and upper body bare. He then took a towel and proceeded with the task of washing the disciples' feet.

In the ancient Middle East it was appropriate, because of custom and from necessity, to wash feet prior to a meal. In those days people wore sandals over bare feet as they trod over dusty, unpaved roads and paths. It was only fitting that a banquet host or one of his servants would wash the dirty feet of the guests. Since it was customary to have prolonged dinners with people reclining next to others' feet, clean feet greatly improved the all-around comfort of each guest.

The foot-washing task normally went to the slave who was lowest on the social ladder; so it was not an agreeable job. Apparently the room in Jerusalem that Jesus and the twelve had procured to celebrate the Passover supper had no such servant available, and none of the disciples volunteered to wash the others' feet. Likely, none wanted to humble himself in such a way that he would be disqualified from the loftiest position in the kingdom, since the debate about the kingdom was still fresh in everyone's mind.

Therefore, Christ humbly took the initiative and began doing what nobody else in the room was willing to do. As He came with His towel and basin of water to Peter, there must have been somewhat of a silence as the men witnessed the King of Glory undertaking one of the most menial and unpleasant of tasks. But Peter, in his frequent role as spokesman for the group, soon broke the silence.

Simon Peter asked Jesus, "Lord, do You wash my feet?" (v. 6), as if to tell Him, "Lord, You shouldn't be doing this." Jesus' answer—

"What I do you do not realize now; but you shall understand hereafter" (v. 7)—indicated that Peter and the others still did not understand the extent of the Lord's condescension on their behalf (cf. Phil.
2:5-8).

But Peter, in his typically bold fashion, persisted in telling Jesus
it was just not right that He should ever wash his feet. That prompted
our Lord to set the record straight concerning the spiritual meaning
of what He was doing: "If I do not wash you, you have no part with
Me" (v. 8). Christ's meaning is fundamental: Peter and anyone else
who would have a saving relationship with God must have his heart
washed and cleansed by Christ.

Somehow what Peter and his fellow disciples had learned earlier
from Jesus simply was not dovetailing in their minds. They knew He
was "the Christ, the Son of the living God" (Matt. 16:16) who had
come "to seek and to save that which was lost" (Luke 19:10). They
had witnessed His power in various miracles. And they had heard
Him teach that He would have to die (John 12:24-25, 32-33). Yet they
were having difficulty accepting all those truths, especially their
Lord's execution on a cross, and grasping all the implications.

But Peter persevered in his quest to understand what Jesus was
saying. He did an about-face and insisted that Christ wash "not my
feet only, but also my hands and my head" (v. 9). He definitely wanted
a relationship with Christ, but he was still unclear regarding exactly
what he needed from the Lord at that moment. Therefore, Jesus further illuminated the spiritual significance of His actions: "He who has
bathed needs only to wash his feet, but is completely clean; and you
are clean" (v. 10).

Essentially Jesus was saying there was a time when all of us who
are believers experienced the washing of regeneration. That's when we
were spiritually washed from head to toe and our sins were completely
cleansed. But as we walk through the world and become contaminated
with the dust and dirt of a sinful society, we need the daily confession,
repentance, and cleansing that keep our feet clean and allow us to have
fellowship with Christ and faithfully carry out His will.

Jesus' words also affirmed to Peter that he had been truly saved and cleansed from his sins. He did not need another bath, but just the constant spiritual foot cleansing that would maintain his walk with the Lord.

Jesus then finished the job of washing the other disciples' feet, at which point He summarized the overall significance of His actions (vv. 12-16). This was a profound object lesson in how love acts. He had loved them to the end, to the maximum, which means He humbly displayed selfless sacrifice and met their needs at the lowliest, most basic level. That selflessness would soon go beyond foot washing to His supreme act of love—His death on the cross, when He would bear their sins and ours, including all those sins of indifference and selfishness that frequently make us so unlovable. Obviously, Jesus' attitude of love, so clearly demonstrated in His actions, can overcome even the greatest resistance sinners can mount against it.

THE APPLICATION OF GENUINE LOVE

Even though Jesus defines foot washing as an example of love the disciples should follow (John 13:15), He spells out perhaps His clearest application of love in John 13:34-35, "A new commandment I give to you, that you love one another, even as I have loved you, that you also love one another. By this all men will know that you are My disciples, if you have love for one another."

We are simply to follow Jesus' pattern and love others by sacrificially meeting their needs. And we are to do so apart from mere emotional impulses and warm feelings, regardless of the human attractiveness the recipients of our love might possess (or lack).

Above all, following Jesus' pattern of genuine love requires true selflessness, which goes against the tide of everything modern culture holds dear. As you might infer from our earlier discussion of the present culture war, western society is extremely self-absorbed, probably more so than at any time in history. People are totally focused on their own needs and desires, always talking about love but understanding nothing of its real meaning. They define love primarily in sexual terms and see it as constantly taking, but seldom as giving. So the challenge for believers is, how can real love shine forth in the midst of such a dark culture?

Our Lord answers that question in John 13:35, "By this all men will know that you are My disciples, if you have love for one another." If the Body of Christ is to be conformed to the image of Christ, and it is (cf. Eph. 3:16-21), then its members must demonstrate the love He has shown to them and sacrifice themselves for each other. That could mean everything from foot washing, manifested in practical acts of service, to giving up our lives. Giving up a life does not necessarily mean dying for someone either. But it might involve devoting the remainder of a life in caring for a disabled spouse or other close family member.

One of the most memorable and encouraging letters I have ever received as a pastor came from a young woman who was a student at the University of Southern California and taught a Sunday school class at Grace Community Church. Here's how she described her profound change of heart toward the young girls she taught:

> I have a class of junior-aged girls. I kept telling myself I loved them, I loved their little curls and I loved their little smiles and I loved their pretty dresses. I just loved the fact that they were sweet little girls. And then one day I came to the realization that I was spending about ten minutes preparing my lesson and I realized that I didn't love them at all because I made no sacrifice to bring them the greatest gift that I could bring them, which was the truth of God's Word. I got on my knees before God and confessed my unloving attitude. I had emotional feelings for those sweet little girls. I didn't love them. Love means preparing diligently to give them my best, even if it meant I couldn't go to the football game, or some other campus activity.

That's an excellent illustration of how one college student, with God's help, came to understand the biblical meaning of love. And it exemplifies the kind of approach all Christians must take if they want their lives to manifest a sincere and godly attitude of love.

5

UNITY: PERSEVERANCE IN THE TRUTH

Nothing is more shattering or devastating to a family than internal discord. All kinds of sin can cause it: pride, selfishness, anger, bitterness, envy, covetousness, and so on. And if these sins can ruin families, marriages, business relationships, or friendships, they can most certainly undermine or destroy the unity of the church. As a pastor and church leader, there is nothing more frightening to view than the above-mentioned sins intensified by a competitive spirit and personality conflicts, causing disharmony and disunity among Christians.

If believers were consistently diligent in pursuing the scriptural character pillars of faith, obedience, humility, and love, the devotion to unity would be automatic. But in the real world where the church functions, unity is very fragile and always susceptible to disruption. As we saw with the attitude of love, the good that God establishes will always be the target of Satan's destructive attacks.

The devil uses believers' sinfulness to foster disunity within the church. When two or more people insist on having things their way, individual priorities will eventually conflict, and arguments will result. Church unity cannot possibly exist if its members' goals, purposes, and ideals are driven by personal egos.

Such quarrelsome disunity among Christians can wreak all sorts of harm. God is displeased and dishonored, the church is discredited and demoralized, and the world is disillusioned and confirmed in its unbelief. Such negative results are not worth the price the church must pay just so a few arrogant believers can fulfill their ego. It's imperative that unity be preserved.

PAUL'S INSTRUCTIONS ON UNITY

The apostle Paul had much firsthand experience with the problem of disunity in the church. Most of the first three chapters of 1 Corinthians deals with factionalism and discord within the Corinthian church. Paul knew the harm such infighting could cause (1 Cor. 3:1-4), and therefore it is logical that he would exhort believers at Ephesus and everywhere to maintain unity: "being diligent to preserve the unity of the Spirit in the bond of peace. There is one body and one Spirit, just as also you were called in one hope of your calling; one Lord, one faith, one baptism, one God and Father of all who is over all and through all and in all" (Eph. 4:3-6).

The maintenance of true spiritual unity should be the continual concern of every believer. The Greek word translated "being diligent" (v. 3) basically means to make haste, and in this context it denotes having a diligent and holy zeal. This striving to keep unity, therefore, is not something to be taken for granted or pursued only casually and periodically.

The unity Paul speaks of is not man-made, not created by a church, not the work of certain denominations or ecumenical movements. He is referring to the inner unity that binds all true believers together as it works in their lives. It is the unity generated by the Holy Spirit and expressed elsewhere by the apostle: "For by one Spirit we were all baptized into one body, whether Jews or Greeks, whether slaves or free, and we were all made to drink of one Spirit. . . . there are many members, but one body" (1 Cor. 12:13, 20; cf. Rom. 8:9). And that unity is held together by the "bond of peace," which is a spiritual belt that surrounds and binds believers together (cf. Phil. 2:2; Col. 3:14).

In contrast, the unbelieving world knows nothing of the true unity that God's Spirit can give (cf. Isa. 48:22). Human statutes, treaties, and agreements cannot produce real peace and unity. As long as the world emphasizes self-centered feelings, prestige, and rights, true harmony will never be achieved.

Paul further emphasizes the definition of spiritual unity in Ephesians 4:4-6 by listing the features that are most relevant to authentic Christian doctrine and practice. Without understanding and embracing these inner, spiritual aspects of unity, believers can never experience it practically. These crucial features are spelled out quite simply in the perfect unity the Trinity promotes.

Unity in the Holy Spirit

The true church is made up of every believer who ever has or will trust in Jesus Christ for salvation. It is one body of saints with no sectarian, ethnic, or geographical divisions. It deserves only the name "Body of Christ," not any label man might want to attach to it.

Every believer is indwelt by the one and only Holy Spirit of God who holds the church together. Each is an individual temple of the Spirit (1 Cor. 3:16-17), "being fitted together . . . growing into a holy temple in the Lord . . . being built together into a dwelling of God in the Spirit" (Eph. 2:21-22). The Holy Spirit is a divine "pledge" (Eph. 1:14) who guarantees that every Christian will be at the marriage supper of the Lamb (Rev. 19:9).

If you are a believer, you are also united with other believers "in one hope of your calling" (Eph. 4:4). The Holy Spirit calls you to salvation, but He also calls you to Christlike maturity (Rom. 8:29; Eph. 1:4), which would include a commitment to unity. There are different spiritual gifts, various ministries, and many places where we can serve God, but just one calling.

Unity in Christ and His Doctrine

It is also clear that we have but "one Lord" (Eph. 4:5), our Savior, Jesus Christ. The apostle Peter also emphasized this in one of his early sermons: "There is salvation in no one else; for there is no other name under heaven that has been given among men, by which we must be saved" (Acts 4:12). Paul not only reiterated that truth to the Ephesians (4:5), but he also assured the Roman church of it: "For the same Lord is Lord of all, abounding in riches for all who call upon Him" (Rom. 10:12).

Because there is only one Lord and Savior, there is also just one true body of doctrine revealed by Him in the New Testament. This is what Jude refers to when, for the sake of preventing discord and disruption within the church, he urges us to "contend earnestly for the faith which was once for all delivered to the saints" (Jude 3). If, with the Lord's help, we faithfully and carefully study His Word, without the undermining influences of the world, blind tradition, or personal biases, we will prevent the body of doctrine from being fragmented into competing and contradictory ideas that inevitably lead to disharmony in the church. Scripture does contain many individual truths, but they are harmonious facets of Christ's one truth, which is our "one faith" (Eph. 4:5).

When we understand that we are united by "one Lord" into "one faith," we will testify to that unity by means of "one baptism." There is without question just one true spiritual baptism, implied in Ephesians 4:4, by which all believers are placed into the Body of Christ. But there is also one water baptism (Eph. 4:5), the common New Testament way of publicly confessing faith in Jesus Christ and solidarity with Him. Believers are not to be baptized in the name of a local church, an influential elder, a famous evangelist, or even the greatest apostle, but only in the name of Christ (1 Cor. 1:13-17).

Unity in God the Father

The foundational, monotheistic doctrine of Judaism is "The LORD is our God, the LORD is one!" (Deut. 6:4), and that oneness is also basic to Christianity, as stated in 1 Corinthians 8:4-6 and James 2:19. Paul's comprehensive statement in Ephesians 4:6, "one God and Father of all who is over all and through all and in all" refers to the magnificent, eternal unity that God gives Christians by His Spirit through the Son. The apostle's point in Ephesians 4 is to refer to the unique roles of each member of the Trinity and yet note their unity within the Godhead and the fact that their unity sovereignly, lovingly, and powerfully holds the church together as one people.

Unity in the Purity of Truth

The implication of all that Paul says in Ephesians 4:3-6, in addition to the essential truth that the church must maintain its unity, is that believers must unite around the truth, and never at the expense of purity or doctrinal clarity. They must strive for a unity that is based on a common understanding of who God is and what His will is, derived from a common understanding of Scripture.

However, there are two broad tendencies within the mainstream evangelical church today that undermine the concept of unity based on purity. One is an ecumenism that says everyone who *claims* to follow Christ is part of one body, no matter how much some of them ignore sound doctrine and hold to certain errors and heresies. Such reasoning says we need to get beyond "inconsequential" doctrinal differences and just enjoy one another and work together at every opportunity. But if it is not based on a genuine, saving faith in the Lord Jesus Christ, that is a phony unity because it is not based on truth.

The other harmful tendency is to overlook sinful behaviors and attitudes and embrace everyone within the church's shadow, no matter how disobedient they are to God's Word. But the apostle Paul, on several occasions, taught that Christian unity does not welcome such people. Titus 3:9-11 says, "But shun foolish controversies and genealogies and strife and disputes about the Law; for they are unprofitable and worthless. Reject a factious man after a first and second warning, knowing that such a man is perverted and is sinning, being self-condemned." A heretic who does not repent forfeits any right to be accepted within the unity of the church's fellowship. Furthermore, Paul told the Thessalonians: "Now we command you, brethren, in the name of our Lord Jesus Christ, that you keep aloof from every brother who leads an unruly life and not according to the tradition which you received from us" (2 Thess. 3:6). The "tradition" mentioned here was not some rabbinic or other man-made rules, but the body of faith and practice revealed to Paul by God's Spirit.

The point here is that true unity of the Spirit belongs only to those who affirm God's truth and live godly lives as a result. If there are individuals in our local churches who persist in teaching error or who refuse to repent from sinful lifestyles, we who are walking with the Lord cannot have fellowship with them.

CHRIST'S CONCERN FOR UNITY

In spite of what Scripture teaches regarding genuine unity's basis in doctrinal and moral purity, many in today's church still don't understand the scriptural definition of unity. They will readily point to John 17:21— "that they may all be one; even as Thou, Father, art in Me, and I in Thee, that they also may be in Us; that the world may believe that Thou didst send Me"—as if to say, "Jesus was concerned at all costs that Christians be unified." However, that is an inaccurate interpretation of that verse.

John 17:21 is part of our Lord's High Priestly Prayer, which encompasses all of chapter 17. When Jesus prays, "that they may all be one," He is not asking that everybody who becomes a Christian will get along well with everybody who professes a like faith. It's not as though He is merely wishing for some sort of unity in the church, which He then asks God to accomplish, only to be disappointed that down through the centuries His prayer has gone unanswered. On the contrary, if Christ prayed for oneness, we can be certain it came to pass! Jesus' prayer is not about how we should all get along externally, but that we in the church will be made one internally.

Marcus Rainsford, a British pastor who helped promote several London evangelistic campaigns of Americans D. L. Moody and Ira Sankey in the late 1800s, provides this additional insight into the purpose of Jesus' great prayer:

> We need to be reminded that our Lord's prayer is not the origin of the union of which He speaks, or the cause of it; but the fruit and result of it. He is not praying that a union might be established between Himself and His people which hitherto had not existed, but that the union which

was always in the mind and purpose and heart of God, and on the ground of which Christ came down to be the Saviour, and the Holy Ghost to be the Comforter, *should be enjoyed* and manifested by His believing people. He would by His words scatter heavenly light round about them, and within them, that they might walk in the light as He Himself was in the light, and as the beloved apostle teaches us in his First Epistle that thus we might have "fellowship . . . with the Father, and with his Son Jesus Christ" (I John 1:3). (*Our Lord Prays for His Own* [1895; Chicago: Moody Press, 1950, 1978], 386-387; emphasis in original)

Jesus' prayer for believers' unity, which He reiterated in John 17:23, is therefore for all those who come to Him to be given the same eternal life, to become partakers of the divine nature, and to have the indwelling of the Spirit of God. Any individual who comes to Christ becomes one with Him; and because he shares His life, he shares the same spiritual life with every other believer. This reality is also clearly spelled out by the apostle Paul: "But one and the same Spirit works all these things, distributing to each one individually just as He wills. For even as the body [of Christ] is one and yet has many members, and all the members of the body, though they are many, are one body, so also is Christ. For by one Spirit we were all baptized [immersed] into one body, whether Jews or Greeks, whether slaves or free, and we were all made to drink of one Spirit. . . . But now there are many members, but one body" (1 Cor. 12:11-13, 20).

THE PRACTICAL OUTWORKING OF UNITY

Jesus' prayer in John 17 has been answered inasmuch as all true believers are one in Him. And this spiritually organic unity—our "like precious faith" (2 Pet. 1:1, KJV)—becomes the basis of our practical, common fellowship. So for the church, genuine and God-given unity is already present. It is not a unity that we who make up the church need to expend great amounts of time and energy trying to generate. But it is a pillar of truth we must hold firmly and preserve with all diligence.

If we properly maintain the precious unity that is ours, the world will see practical manifestations of it. And in that way unbelievers can hardly receive a more credible testimony to the truth of the Gospel. The apostle Paul's instructions to the Corinthian church on how to practically demonstrate unity are crystal-clear: "Now I exhort you, brethren, by the name of our Lord Jesus Christ, that you all agree, and there be no divisions among you, but you be made complete in the same mind and in the same judgment" (1 Cor. 1:10).

Doctrinal Unity

Paul's statement in 1 Corinthians, in contrast to what we saw in Ephesians 4:3-6 and its emphasis on the mystical unity of the universal Body of Christ, stresses the unity of the local church, which today looms as a seemingly impossible standard for many churches. But God, through His Spirit, gives us the power to fulfill commands that are humanly impossible—for example, Christ's command that all believers "be perfect, as your heavenly Father is perfect" (Matt. 5:48). That high level of maturity and sanctification is attainable, and so is the goal that members of a local church be in agreement about the things of God.

The apostle's order in 1 Corinthians 1:10 "that you all agree" is more helpfully translated by the *King James Version's* literal "that ye all speak the same thing." It is potentially confusing and spiritually detrimental for inquiring unbelievers and new believers alike to hear supposedly mature and knowledgeable Christians teach conflicting things about the Gospel, Scripture, or principles of Christian living. It is also harmful if everyone speaks his own opinions about certain doctrines. That can result in the emergence of factions, each vocally expressing its own viewpoint and criticizing everyone else.

If a local church wants to have a vibrant and effective ministry, it must speak with one voice on *essential* doctrinal matters. And its instruction must not be offered as items on a menu, from which members choose what appeals to them and ignore or criticize what does not. Unfortunately, too many churches, Christian colleges and seminaries, and evangelical ministries have that sort of doctrinal and ethical selectivity. They might present a facade of social and organizational unity, but when it comes to teaching doctrinal and biblical certainties, they waver and communicate mixed signals. Of course, holding to absolutes and being dogmatic about theology or ethics is not popular today. Most people, including more and more professing Christians, are averse to such definite standards. For one thing, many want to avoid the specific application and obedience that a definite solidarity and conviction on doctrine requires.

With God's truth, there simply can't be two conflicting views. Granted, we can't and shouldn't be dogmatic about what is not fully or clearly revealed (Deut. 29:29). But God does not disagree with Himself, and portions of Scripture do not disagree with other portions. Thus Paul tells the Corinthians, and all Christians, that they must have doctrinal unity—a unity that is based clearly, completely, and only on the inspired Word of God.

The apostle's call for doctrinal agreement therefore has certain distinctives. It is based on Scripture, which was given by and fulfilled in Jesus Christ ("by the name of our Lord Jesus Christ") and was completed through the apostles' teachings. Paul's call is to a standard that applies to all groups of believers: "Let us therefore, as many as are perfect, have this attitude; and if in anything you have a different attitude, God will reveal that also to you; however, let us keep living by that same standard to which we have attained" (Phil. 3:15-16). His standard was the apostolic doctrine that he personally taught and exemplified to the churches (e.g., v. 17; 1 Cor. 2:4).

Avoiding Divisions

Paul also urged the Corinthian church and all others to avoid divisions; otherwise, none of the unity and agreement he desired would occur. The Greek *schismata*, which gives us the English *schism*, is the word translated "divisions" in 1 Corinthians 1:10 and means literally "to tear or rip." In its broader meaning it signifies a divided judgment, a difference of opinion, or a dissension. The Gospel of John uses it to describe the differing evaluations the people on one occasion had of Jesus: "There arose a division [*schisma*] in the multitude because of Him" (7:43).

In line with our discussion of unity's practical implications, the most serious divisions are those that occur over doctrine and thus destroy a church's unity in Christ. There is absolutely no place in a church for teaching and activity that divides the people over a matter that is clearly taught in the Word. People who engage in such serious divisiveness actually are self-serving and should be marked out and shunned, as Paul warned the church in Rome: "Now I urge you, brethren, keep your eye on those who cause dissensions and hindrances contrary to the teaching which you learned, and turn away from them" (Rom. 16:17).

One important way a church can prevent major divisions is to have godly leadership that is well-taught in the Word, Spirit-led, and united on what God's will is for the church. Such men know and agree upon sound doctrine and will have the discernment to recognize when seeds of discord and error are being sown and the ability to stop such destructive activity. Godly leaders will consistently lead a church in the biblical unity of faith and practice (cf. Heb. 13:7), and they should be followed and supported (1 Thess. 5:12-13; Heb. 13:17).

Complete Unity

Paul concludes 1 Corinthians 1:10 with this mandate: "Be made complete in the same mind and in the same judgment." "Made complete" refers to putting something back together in one piece—to repair something that was broken or separated. Genuine believers who are part of a church are to be "perfectly joined together" (as the KJV translates the word rendered "made complete" in the NASB), both inwardly ("in the same mind") and outwardly ("in the same judgment").

Having those attitudes excludes a reluctant or phony form of unity. True unity will not say the same thing publicly while privately harboring disagreements and objections. That kind of hypocrisy might not hinder a church's size, but it will lessen its effectiveness.

Anyone who takes such a stance and strongly disagrees with his local assembly's doctrine and direction won't experience much personal spiritual growth and will not be of great service to his church.

We're not saying, however, that believers are to be photocopies of one another. God has created each of us as unique individuals with different personalities, interests, skills, and spiritual gifts. No church, no matter how sound, will see all its members agree on every single issue that the leaders suggest or implement. There is not absolute unanimity in the congregation at my church over every little thing that happens, but that is beside the point. The priority is for everyone to lovingly sacrifice their personal opinions on nonessential or less important matters for the sake of overall unity. As we have said, the crucial element in displaying a practical Christian unity for those around us is that we be of the same mind concerning basic doctrine, lifestyle, and church policy.

Spiritual unity biblically expressed has always been God's will for His people, and it will always be a blessing to them and a potentially effective witness to those outside the church. Genuine unity for believers was God's will in the Old Testament: "Behold, how good and how pleasant it is for brothers to dwell together in unity" (Ps. 133:1). And we have seen in various New Testament passages the great concern the Lord Jesus and the apostle Paul had for believers to realize and live out the unity God's Spirit has granted them. Oneness among Christians was again Paul's concern at the conclusion of his teaching to the Romans on liberty of conscience: "Now may the God who gives perseverance and encouragement grant you to be of the same mind with one another according to Christ Jesus; that with one accord you may with one voice glorify the God and Father of our Lord Jesus Christ. Wherefore, accept one another, just as Christ also accepted us to the glory of God" (Rom. 15:5-7).

That passage contains another reference to the "mind," which further verifies the truth that the outworking of our organic spiritual unity, the demonstration of God's indwelling Spirit in our lives, starts with the mind. The Christian faith is a cognitive faith; therefore, we don't need to maintain unity by inducing some kind of emotional hysteria or sentimentalism in which we rally around a common cause and hypnotically merge ourselves into one group. Instead, God wants us to rationally express unity, centered on a common understanding of His revealed truth.

Christians could spend a lifetime trying to unify themselves, and it would all be futile if they didn't look to a common standard. As pastor and Christian writer A. W. Tozer used to illustrate, if a person had 4,000 pianos and tried to tune them to each other, he or she would fail. But if the same individual used a tuning fork, he could successfully tune all the pianos to it. And the one tuning fork all believers are tuned to is faith, the truth of the Gospel. When we're all tuned to that, we're all tuned to each other. Apart from a Spirit-informed understanding of the truth, accompanied by a pursuit of godliness that regularly and continually deals with sin, we will not realize the Christian character-pillar of unity in our fellowship. But if we do unite in the pursuit of truth and holiness (Rom. 15:6; 1 Cor. 1:10; Phil. 1:27), we will minister to one another in harmony, glorify the Lord with one voice, and send a uniform and consistent witness to those who don't know Him.

6

GROWTH:
NO REAL LIFE WITHOUT IT

Life by its very definition is a growth process. That which is alive is growing. For example, seedlings grow to be trees, in some cases to heights of several hundred feet. Even when they reach their full height, they exhibit regular growth through the production of new leaves, branches, or fruit.

The principle of growth also holds true in the spiritual realm. An essential, inherent characteristic for everyone in the Body of Christ is individual spiritual growth. Pastor John R. W. Stott calls spiritual growth a believer's responsibility:

> The great privilege of the child of God is relationship; his great responsibility is growth. Everybody loves children, but nobody in his right mind wants them [to] stay in the nursery. The tragedy, however, is that many Christians, born again in Christ, never grow up. Others even suffer from spiritual infantile regression. Our heavenly Father's purpose, on the other hand, is that "babes in Christ" should become "mature in Christ." Our birth must be followed by growth. The crisis of justification (our acceptance before God) must lead to the process of sanctification (our growth in holiness, what Peter terms "growing up to salvation" [1 Pet. 2:2]). (*Basic Christianity* [Downers Grove, Ill.: InterVarsity Press, 1958], 136)

SPIRITUAL GROWTH IS MANDATORY

It is discouraging and disappointing to know of believers who have not developed or grown in their faith. In the first place, a lack of spiritual growth is unnecessary because God has provided every Christian, through His Word, all the spiritual resources needed for growth. Spiritual growth is essential and possible. Furthermore, it is a command, not an option, as God's Word demonstrates.

In 2 Peter 3:18, the apostle Peter commands all of us who are believers, "But grow in the grace and knowledge of our Lord and Savior Jesus Christ." We are to grow in the sphere of God's grace and in both biblical and experiential knowledge as the Lord works His will through all the challenges of life, both easy and difficult.

However, we are not left solely to our own resources. The apostle Paul writes these words of encouragement: "But we all, with unveiled face beholding as in a mirror the glory of the Lord, are being transformed into the same image from glory to glory, just as from the Lord, the Spirit" (2 Cor. 3:18). Scripture is the mirror, and as we open the Word, God's glory reflects off and manifests itself to us through the pages. When that happens, genuine spiritual growth takes place, and we "are being transformed into the same image from glory to glory, just as from the Lord, the Spirit." As we faithfully look into His Word, God through the Holy Spirit causes us to grow in ever-increasing levels of maturity toward Christlikeness.

Later, Paul prayed that the Corinthians would "be made complete" (2 Cor. 13:9). He wanted them to advance all the way to the pinnacle of complete spiritual maturity. The apostle earnestly desired such growth for all believers. In Galatians 4:19 (NIV) he wrote, "My dear children, for whom I am again in the pains of childbirth until Christ is formed in you . . ." In Ephesians it was his desire that the believers grow "until we all attain to the unity of the faith, and of the knowledge of the Son of God, to a mature man, to the measure of the stature which belongs to the fulness of Christ" (Eph. 4:13).

When he wrote to the Philippians, Paul had been a believer for thirty years, and yet he knew that he and all other believers were continually being called to spiritual maturity: "Brethren, I do not regard myself as having laid hold of it yet; but one thing I do: forgetting what lies behind and reaching forward to what lies ahead, I press on toward the goal for the prize of the upward call of God in Christ Jesus" (Phil. 3:13-14). And this ongoing command has no middle ground, no place of neutrality—we are either growing spiritually or we are regressing. The price for regressing is inevitably that we have to regain spiritual ground—ground that we once gained but now have lost. Therefore the ideal is that we obey Paul's words to Timothy and "pursue [keep growing in] righteousness, godliness, faith, love, perseverance and gentleness" (1 Tim. 6:11).

LEVELS OF SPIRITUAL MATURITY

The command that all believers grow spiritually is straightforward in Scripture, as 1 John 2:12-14 demonstrates: "I am writing to you, little children, because your sins are forgiven you for His name's sake. I am writing to you, fathers, because you know Him who has been from the beginning. I am writing to you, young men, because you have overcome the evil one. I have written to you, children, because you know the Father. I have written to you, fathers, because you know Him who has been from the beginning. I have written to you, young men, because you are strong, and the word of God abides in you, and you have overcome the evil one." The apostle John clearly calls everyone whose sins have been forgiven "little children" (v. 12). Since all genuine believers—because they've repented of sin and trusted in Christ's work on the cross—have had their sins forgiven, it is logical to conclude that they may all be called by the endearing expression "little children."

That passage also reveals three basic stages of spiritual growth. First there are "children" (v. 13), who are different from the children of verse 12. John refers to a subcategory of believers by using a word that means "spiritual infants." Then he mentions two more-advanced levels of development, "young men" and "fathers."

Spiritual Infants

As any parent would attest, one truism of infants and little children is their lack of discernment about what is or isn't good for them. When my young grandchildren visit our house, they don't beg for carrots or some other nutritious snack—they would rather have a candy bar. Toddlers lack discrimination about what's beneficial for them. As they walk around their homes, they will put any accessible item into their mouths or try to explore any area, no matter how dangerous. They are absolutely undiscerning and not yet trained enough to recognize life's hazards.

Spiritual infants, either new believers or immature Christians, also lack discernment. Ephesians 4:13-14 calls us to maturity and discernment: "until we all attain to the unity of the faith, and of the knowledge of the Son of God, to a mature man, to the measure of the stature which belongs to the fulness of Christ. As a result, we are no longer to be children, tossed here and there by waves, and carried about by every wind of doctrine, by the trickery of men, by craftiness in deceitful scheming."

When anyone still struggling in their spiritual infancy begins to deepen their knowledge of Jesus Christ (v. 13), he will eventually progress from his childish level of understanding to a greater level of maturity. And how is that childish level defined? Paul says it is when the individual is "tossed here and there by waves, and carried about by every wind of doctrine, by the trickery of men, by craftiness in deceitful scheming" (v. 14). That summarizes the problem with spiritual infancy—a lack of discernment and a vulnerability to doctrinal error. False teachers find it easy to seduce spiritual babies by perverting the truth. Therefore, it's essential that new Christians be integrated into the life of a strong church where they will be well fed from the Word and thoroughly protected from potential spiritual harm.

So the dominant negative characteristic of the spiritual infant is lack of discernment. But 1 John 2:13 does identify a positive characteristic: "I have written to you, children, because you know the Father." The first thing parents usually hear—and hope to hear—

from the mouth of their young child is some word that sounds at least remotely similar to "Mama" or "Dada." In spite of the many things young children do not yet know or understand, they do know and recognize their parents, whom they look to for food, warmth, love, and protection.

Similarly, the new believer knows the Lord is his source of joy and blessing in his new life. But again, unless he is protected from harmful and destructive doctrinal influences, his joy will soon disappear. To rejoice in a basic knowledge of Jesus' love is a wonderful starting point for God's children, but they all need to press on in the goal to be more like Christ.

Spiritual Youth

As believers mature beyond spiritual infancy, they reach a second level of maturity, what the apostle John calls "young men," who "have overcome the evil one" (1 John 2:13). The Greek for "have overcome" is in the perfect tense, which means we can reach a point in our spiritual development where we have already overcome the evil one, Satan. And this victory will have ongoing results in our life.

Overcoming Satan, however, is not the same thing as getting rid of sin. Satan may prod us and, through his world-centered system, place many temptations in our paths, but he is not directly making us commit wicked deeds. Instead, the devil is much more involved in the development of deceptive, ungodly, antibiblical ideologies. He was a liar from the beginning (John 8:44; cf. Gen. 3:4) and is busy developing all kinds of lies—various ideologies, philosophies, religions, and all sorts of deceptive schemes (cf. 2 Cor. 10:3-5; 11:14) to blind unregenerate people and render spiritual infants ineffective. Satan can't take away young believers' salvation, but he can certainly keep them in spiritual infancy and prevent them from having any positive impact for the kingdom of God.

The only way to overcome Satan is to be strong in the knowledge of Scripture: "I have written to you, young men, because you are strong, and the word of God abides in you, and you have overcome the evil one" (1 John 2:14). If you reach this level of maturity, you will still have sin and temptation in your life, but you will also know sound doctrine well enough to recognize error, resist its enticements, and fight it vigorously when it confronts you or others.

As Christians mature, they are able to understand and correctly interpret the Word of God. As a result, their theology starts to take shape as they acquire discernment by asking the right questions. With their increased doctrinal knowledge comes a desire to discuss Scripture and theology with more learned believers so they can be more active in refuting the cults and all forms of doctrinal error.

Growing into effective spiritual young men and women is simply a matter of knowing the truth (2 Pet. 3:18). We increase our understanding and gain spiritual muscle as we study the Scriptures, just as going to a health club and working out will make us stronger and give us seemingly boundless amounts of physical strength and energy.

As you mature as a spiritual youth, you will possess a vigorous and passionate drive for the truth because your theology is coming into focus. You can use the Word to discern the times and trends in our society and thereby deal with the important life issues all around us. You will believe, know, and understand what the Bible teaches about the great redemptive truths that dominate God's Word. In that sense you'll stand on firm ground and be strong.

Spiritual Fathers

As uplifting as the Christian life can be during the previous level of growth, that is not where our maturing should end. John twice identifies a third category of development in 1 John 2:13-14: "I am writing to you, fathers. . . . I have written to you, fathers." There is a clear difference between this last level of maturity and the previous one. Whereas the spiritual youth is excited about pulling his biblical and doctrinal knowledge together and vigorously applying it to every issue, the spiritual father (man or woman) has a certain sense of rest, tranquillity, and depth of character. The reason for such peace is repeated by John in verses 13 and 14: "because you know Him who has been from the beginning."

The apostle is saying that the most mature believers will begin to have a deeper knowledge of God. This is not some kind of mystical experience, but an understanding of Scripture that becomes deeper and richer as they progress from knowing facts and principles to knowing the God who revealed Himself through the words of Scripture. Knowing the Father more intimately involves such things as experiencing enough answered prayers that there's no doubt He does hear and answer, and experiencing enough of life's sufferings and trials to realize that God is always there to sustain and comfort.

Those who have reached the level of spiritual fathers will exhibit characteristics that A. W. Tozer has described:

> A Christian is spiritual [mature] when he sees everything from God's viewpoint. The ability to weigh all things in the divine scale and place the same value upon them as God does is the mark of a Spirit-filled life.
>
> God looks *at* and *through* at the same time. His gaze does not rest on the surface but penetrates to the true meaning of things. The carnal [immature] Christian looks at an object or a situation, but because he does not see through it he is elated or cast down by what he sees. The spiritual man is able to look through things as God looks and think of them as God thinks. He insists on seeing all things as God sees them even if it humbles him and exposes his ignorance to the point of real pain. (*That Incredible Christian*, "Marks of the Spiritual Man," in *The Best of A. W. Tozer*, compiled by Warren W. Wiersbe [Grand Rapids, Mich.: Baker, 1978], 113, emphasis in the original)

There's a settled character and a depth to those who really know their God. And the Bible says they will do great things for Him (Dan. 11:32). That's where all believers should ultimately desire to be.

The key to reaching that ultimate level of maturity is to recognize and remember the crucial role obedience plays. The various levels of maturity are not absolute guarantees; they are linked to obedience. At any stage of our spiritual development we can either be obeying God or the flesh. That means that whether we're spiritual infants, spiritual youth, or spiritual fathers, we can either be progressing in spiritual maturity or regressing. We cannot and must not rest in our perceived level of growth, thinking we're automatically mature when in reality our maturity is based on whether or not we're obeying God. Spiritual maturity, then, is the process that moves believers from being spiritual infants to spiritual youth to spiritual fathers during, and only during, those experiences in their lives when they walk in the Spirit and obey God's Word.

SCRIPTURE: THE KEY TO GROWTH

One of the sad realities in the contemporary church is that more and more often the careful, thoughtful, precise interpretation of God's Word is being depreciated in favor of subjective and mystical "spiritual experiences." As a result, many professed believers are not growing at all. It's as if a group of people ate nothing but junk food. Those who get caught up in empty and superficial experiences are pursuing a path that leads to error and that cannot produce real spiritual change and growth. In effect, they're missing the genuine path to maturity, which comes by means of God's Word. They are content to remain at a basic level of immaturity, accompanied by all sorts of problems and deceptions, rather than progressing in the levels of maturity.

The classic text on the Word's power, value, and importance in the believer's maturing process is 2 Timothy 3:15-17, which says, "From childhood you have known the sacred writings which are able to give you the wisdom that leads to salvation through faith which is in Christ Jesus. All Scripture is inspired by God and profitable for teaching, for reproof, for correction, for training in righteousness; that the man of God may be adequate, equipped for every good work." This passage, more succinctly than any other in the New Testament, outlines the spiritually transforming power of the Word.

Scripture's Role in Salvation

Timothy was privileged to first hear the Word at an early age (2 Tim. 3:15), because "from childhood" his grandmother Lois and his mother Eunice had taught him "the sacred writings"—the Old Testament (see 2 Tim. 1:5). They built their faith and devotion on those writings and helped Timothy do the same. As they all became exposed to New Testament truth, the Old Testament's anticipation of salvation turned into a firm realization. They had repented under the grace and mercy of the God of Abraham, Isaac, and Jacob; when they heard the Gospel of Jesus Christ, they knew God's promise of the Messiah-Redeemer had been fulfilled, and they trusted Him as Lord and Savior.

Paul exhorted Timothy, who was more easily intimidated and discouraged than the apostle, to hold on and stand firm in what he had learned. Both in his family and under Paul's leadership, Timothy became sound in his knowledge of Scripture. Paul did not need to admonish him about faulty doctrine or sin but urged him to persevere in the truth and the sound doctrine he already knew.

Paul, like our Lord before him (John 5:39), clarifies the fact that the words of Scripture themselves—or an intellectual knowledge thereof—do not grant salvation, but rather "the wisdom" they impart "leads to salvation through faith which is in Christ Jesus."

Thus, the first work the Word does is bring believers to salvation (cf. Ps. 19:7; Mark 4:14-20; John 5:24, 39; Jas. 1:18; 1 Pet. 1:23). The truth of Scripture, when mixed with faith in Christ and energized by the Holy Spirit, leads to spiritual life. The apostle Paul asked the Romans, "How shall they [unbelievers] hear without a preacher?" (Rom. 10:14) and later explained that "faith comes from hearing, and hearing by the word of Christ" (v. 17).

Scripture's Role in Teaching

Second Timothy 3:16 delineates how the Word works in maturing believers, beginning with its teaching role. Paul says it is "profitable for teaching." "Profitable" (the Greek word can be translated "beneficial" or "productive") focuses on the sufficiency of Scripture. This means Scripture is comprehensive, absolutely able to meet believers' every spiritual need (cf. Josh. 1:8; Ps. 119).

"Teaching" simply means that the Word conveys doctrine, not dogmatism, by which believers come to understand God's mind, which encompasses His truth, His principles, His law, His requirements, and His commands. All are foundational for every facet of Christian living.

The important point regarding Scripture's essential role in teaching is that apart from it there are certain truths we could never know about God. Everyone can know something about God through His general revelation, by which He reveals His wisdom and the power, variety, and magnificence in His creation and that He is a personal God. But God's saving love cannot be known apart from special revelation. Paul explains it this way:

> *Just as it is written, "Things which eye has not seen and ear has not heard, and which have not entered the heart of man, all that God has prepared for those who love Him." For to us God revealed them through the Spirit; for the Spirit searches all things, even the depths of God. . . . But a natural man does not accept the things of the Spirit of God; for they are foolishness to him, and he cannot understand them, because they are spiritually appraised. But he who is spiritual appraises all things, yet he himself is appraised by no man. For who has known the mind of the Lord, that he should instruct Him? But we have the mind of Christ.*
> *—1 Cor. 2:9-10, 14-16*

The truths that pertain to genuine spiritual life and Christian maturity are simply unavailable to and cannot be understood by unbelievers. Such matters can't be grasped empirically or philosophically; they're not available internally or externally by human wisdom. The only way anyone will ever know the things of God is by the Holy Spirit's instruction through the revealed Word (John 14:16-17; 16:13; 1 John 2:20, 24, 27). That is what Jesus said sanctifies all believers: "Sanctify them in the truth; Thy word is truth" (John 17:17).

Scripture's Role in Reproof

Once God's Word begins to teach believers the truth, it will eventually and inevitably reprove certain ideas and behaviors. The word "reproof" in 2 Timothy 3:16 means "to rebuke, refute, or convict" misbehavior or false doctrine. Scripture confronts two areas: it exposes sin and refutes error.

God's Word has the negative ministry of destroying and eliminating whatever is sinful and false, just as much as it has the positive ministry of edifying and enhancing whatever is righteous and true. This reproving ministry is how Paul continually used the Word: "I testify to you this day, that I am innocent of the blood of all men. . . . Therefore be on the alert, remembering that night and day for a period of three years I did not cease to admonish each one with tears" (Acts 20:26, 31).

Mature believers who preach or teach the Word will use it to rebuke what is wrong as well as to emphasize what is right. Jesus referred to such a process when He told the disciples, "Every branch in Me that does not bear fruit, He takes away; and every branch that bears fruit, He prunes it, that it may bear more fruit" (John 15:2).

Spiritual growth can blossom as we allow the Word to confront our sin and error and lead us to walk in the Spirit. That is why Scripture's reproof is so profitable. And it is why we should be grateful for its discipline, just like the writer of Proverbs: "For the commandment is a lamp, and the teaching is light; and reproofs for discipline are the way of life" (6:23).

Scripture's Role in Correction

When I was in school, I appreciated those teachers who marked wrong answers on my papers and then wrote in the correct ones. But those who only marked wrong answers without indicating what was correct frustrated me. Scripture is not like those schoolteachers who would merely mark wrong answers. It actually corrects us. The Greek word for "correction" in 2 Timothy 3:16 literally means "to straighten up." God's Word doesn't just rebuke, convict, and refute.

It goes further and pulls us back into line, mending, rebuilding, and fixing what is broken.

Not unlike the relationship parents have with their children, spiritual mothers and fathers reprove their children regarding sins and areas that need improvement. If they are good parents, they will then set their children on the correct path by teaching them appropriate behaviors and attitudes.

Scriptural correction therefore is the positive provision for believers who accept the Word's negative reproof. The process sometimes "for the moment seems not to be joyful, but sorrowful; yet to those who have been trained by it, afterwards it yields the peaceful fruit of righteousness" (Heb. 12:11).

Scripture's Role in Training in Righteousness

If we're allowing God's Word to have an authentic role in our spiritual growth, it will not just leave us with the bare elements of truth. Instead, the Word will apply to our lives what it has taught us so that it might continually build us up in righteousness. In 2 Timothy 3:16 this process is denoted by the Greek word *paideia*, which is rendered "training" and originally meant training a child (*paidion*) but came to have a broader meaning of any sort of training, as it does in this verse.

But how does training in righteousness express itself practically? The process begins when we hear Scripture preached during the worship service or taught in a Sunday school class or Bible study. That's when we store doctrinal and biblical truth in our hearts and minds.

The next practical phase of our training in righteousness comes in our daily lives as we interact with people and ideas of the world and occasionally need to confront error. You might find yourself in a group discussion when someone interjects an obvious doctrinal error. At that point you can draw on Scripture to refute the error and allow the truth to shape the thinking of the other people in the group. In that way you will be obeying the apostle Paul's command to present yourselves "approved to God as a workman who does not need to be ashamed, handling accurately the word of truth" (2 Tim. 2:15; cf. Eph. 6:14-17).

On a more personal level you can be trained in righteousness when you encounter a temptation. When you think you may be on the verge of losing a battle with temptation, you can draw on your knowledge of Scripture to help you respond in a righteous and godly way. Similarly, you may face a major trial in which your understanding of the Word will take over, guide you through the crisis, and thereby further train you in righteousness. Following the example of the Lord Jesus (see Matt. 4:3-10), we need to carefully and accurately use Scripture to deal with each and every temptation or trial from the world (cf. Ps. 119:9-11; Col. 3:16).

No matter how deep our understanding of Scripture is, God still trains us in ways we don't always comprehend. However, that should not keep us from affirming with the psalmist, "As the deer pants for the water brooks, so my soul pants for Thee, O God" (Ps. 42:1).

DESIRING SCRIPTURE

If we are going to experience genuine growth, it must occur according to the pattern of 1 Peter 2:1-2: "Therefore, putting aside all malice [evil] and all guile [deceit] and hypocrisy and envy and all slander, like newborn babes, long for the pure milk of the word, that by it you may grow in respect to salvation."

Verse 1 simply means we must deal with all the sin in our lives by constantly confessing and forsaking it. Then we can get to the heart of the matter in verse 2 and have an unencumbered desire for the richness and purity of Scripture. As David wrote in Psalm 19:10, the Word is "more desirable than gold, yes, than much fine gold; sweeter also than honey and the drippings of the honeycomb." David also wrote in Psalm 1:2 that the righteous person's "delight is in the law [Word] of the LORD, and in His law he meditates day and night." And he stated over and over in Psalm 119 that he delighted in the Word. Such a strong, joyful longing for Scripture is also our foundational key for growing more and more Christlike.

The analogy in 1 Peter 2:2 is very plain. The apostle Peter is simply saying that believers should long for the Word the way a baby longs for milk. In the Greek, the term translated "long for" means an intense, recurring craving, and that's how babies will express their desire for milk. They don't care if it's from a bottle or directly from Mom, what color their room is, or even what time of day it is—they want milk, and if they don't get it soon enough, they scream and cry. Believers should have that same kind of single-minded craving for the Word of God.

Peter doesn't say read the Bible, or study it, or meditate on it—he says *desire* it. It's what Paul calls "the love of the truth" (2 Thess. 2:10). In effect, this produces an attitude in the believer's heart that says, "I want the Word more than I want anything else."

We need that kind of strong desire if we are going to know Scripture well enough so it can train us in righteousness. Consider the passion for truth that the writer of Proverbs outlines:

> *My son, if you will receive my sayings, and treasure my commandments within you, make your ear attentive to wisdom, incline your heart to understanding; for if you cry for discernment, lift your voice for understanding; if you seek her as silver, and search for her as for hidden treasures; then you will discern the fear of the LORD, and discover the knowledge of God. For the LORD gives wisdom; from His mouth come knowledge and understanding.*
>
> *—2:1-6*

If we seek divine truth as earnestly as some people go after material riches, we will find it, because God has made it available (cf. Job 28).

Supposedly a young man once came to the ancient Greek philosopher and teacher Socrates and asked him, "O master Socrates, will you be my teacher?"

Socrates replied, "Follow me," and turned and walked into the sea. He kept walking and walking, and the young man kept following and following. He wanted very much to have the master Socrates as his mentor.

They eventually reached the depth at which the water was just touching their lips. Socrates then turned around and put both hands on the young man's head and pushed him under. The man, wanting to be a compliant student, stayed underwater for a while.

But soon the young man began to spit and sputter and flail around as he gasped for air. All the while Socrates, who apparently was quite strong, held him under the water. Soon the man began blowing large bubbles and thrashing more madly. Finally, Socrates took his hands off his would-be student, who popped to the surface of the water.

Gasping for air and spewing water out of his mouth, the young man frantically asked the philosopher, "Why did you do that? Why?"

Socrates answered him, "When you want to learn as much as you wanted to breathe, I will be your teacher."

When believers want to find and know the truth the way some people look for natural treasures, when believers crave the Word as passionately as an infant craves milk, they will grow and mature and become like Jesus Christ.

Joshua 1:8 provides a fitting summary to our study of spiritual growth: "This book of the law shall not depart from your mouth, but you shall meditate on it day and night, so that you may be careful to do according to all that is written in it; for then you will make your way prosperous, and then you will have [spiritual] success." The key is to absorb God's Word and live it out.

7

FORGIVE AND
BE BLESSED

One essential pillar of Christian character, which can easily be neglected at great harm to the church, is the attitude of forgiveness. It must accompany our unity and pursuit of holiness (spiritual growth); otherwise the Body of Christ can become very harsh, rigid, and bitter, which leads to holding grudges and elevating pride.

Forgiveness is absolutely essential because as much as we would like to bring the perfection of heaven down into the operation of the church, that won't happen in this life. Instead, there will be sins, imperfections, errors, misjudgments, and wrong attitudes, and they will occur among the church leadership as well as in the congregation.

Even the apostle Paul, at the pinnacle of his life and at the very end of his career as a stalwart Christian leader and church planter, identified himself as the foremost of all sinners (1 Tim. 1:15). Sins will always plague us, and we'll constantly be agreeing with Paul's words, "Wretched man that I am! Who will set me free from the body of this death?" (Rom. 7:24). In fact, the longer we follow the pattern of spiritual growth outlined in the last chapter and the more mature we become, the more sensitive we'll be to sin and the more aware we'll be of our failures.

Thus the most mature believers should always sense the need to have a forgiving attitude within the life of the church. Unforgiving attitudes, if not repented of, will invariably lead to a lack of unity and fellowship among believers, a limited usefulness in ministry, and a loss of the joy and peace that all Christians should experience through the Holy Spirit.

Of course, today's secular, psychologically seduced culture, which is bent on exercising and glorifying the sin of self-esteem, mocks forgiveness. People cling tenaciously to their personal "right" to be offended at every supposed wrong they experience. They also take much satisfaction in exacting vengeance on others. All of that is contrary to what Scripture teaches us and is all the more reason Christians must be characterized as forgiving.

THE MOST GODLIKE ACTION

Samuel Davies, an evangelist and the organizer of Presbyterianism in colonial America, wonderfully expressed in the following stanzas of a hymn God's forgiving attitude and what our response should be:

> *Pardon from an offended God!*
> *Pardon for sins of deepest dye!*
> *Pardon bestowed through Jesus' blood!*
> *Pardon that brings the rebel nigh!*
> *Who is a pard'ning God like thee?*
> *Or who has grace so rich and free?*
>
> *O may this glorious, matchless love,*
> *This Godlike miracle of grace,*
> *Teach mortal tongues, like those above,*
> *To raise this song of lofty praise:*
> *Who is a pard'ning God like thee?*
> *Or who has grace so rich and free?*

As those verses suggest, God's forgiveness is marvelous. It is His undeserved, unearned love that does not hold the sinner guilty but completely passes by the transgression. When we manifest forgiveness, we're essentially saying that no matter what someone else has done, we will not remain angry or desire vengeance. We will not blame the other person or feel self-pity because we've been offended. Rather, we are prepared to pass by that sin and fully extend love to that person.

That's forgiveness, and it's a godlike character trait. I am convinced that forgiveness is the most godlike favor we can extend to someone else. If it's our sincere desire to be Christlike, then we must possess and demonstrate the attitude of forgiveness. We are never more like our heavenly Father than when we forgive someone.

God by Nature Forgives

Scripture is replete with evidence that God is a forgiving God. Exodus 34:6-7 says, "Then the LORD passed by in front of him [Moses] and proclaimed, 'The LORD, the LORD God, compassionate and gracious, slow to anger, and abounding in lovingkindness and truth; who keeps lovingkindness for thousands, who forgives iniquity, transgression and sin.'" Moses had asked to see God's glory, so the Lord revealed a small portion of it as He passed by and identified some of His basic nature.

The Psalms also attest to the truth of God's forgiving nature. Here are three representative passages:

How blessed is he whose transgression is forgiven, whose sin is covered! How blessed is the man to whom the LORD does not impute iniquity.

—32:1-2

Thou didst forgive the iniquity of Thy people; Thou didst cover all their sin. Thou didst withdraw all Thy fury; Thou didst turn away from Thy burning anger.

—85:2-3

If Thou, LORD, shouldst mark iniquities, O LORD, who could stand? But there is forgiveness with Thee, that Thou mayest be feared.

—130:3-4

The Old Testament prophets also proclaimed the truth of God's forgiving nature. God spoke through Isaiah and said, "I, even I, am the one who wipes out your transgressions for My own sake; and I will not remember your sins" (Isa. 43:25). God simply says He will put His character as a forgiving God on display and thus receive worship from those who are grateful for His forgiveness.

In Isaiah 55:6-7 the prophet reiterated the principle of forgiveness with the exhortation, "Seek the LORD while He may be found; call upon Him while He is near. Let the wicked forsake his way, and the unrighteous man his thoughts; and let him return to the LORD, and He will have compassion on him; and to our God, for He will abundantly pardon."

In Jeremiah 33:8 God three times states the significance of the people's sins and twice proclaims His attitude of forgiveness: "And I will cleanse them from all their iniquity by which they have sinned against Me, and I will pardon all their iniquities by which they have sinned against Me, and by which they have transgressed against Me."

New Testament Illustrations of Forgiveness

God's essential forgiving nature is perhaps nowhere better portrayed than in Jesus' well-known Parable of the Prodigal Son (which could more appropriately be titled the Parable of the Forgiving Father). Luke 15:11-24 records the compassionate father's dealings with his wayward son:

> *And He said, "A certain man had two sons; and the younger of them said to his father, 'Father, give me the share of the estate that falls to me.' And he divided his wealth between them. And not many days later, the younger son gathered everything together and went on a journey into a distant country, and there he squandered his estate with loose living. Now when he had spent everything, a severe famine occurred in that country, and he began to be in need. And he went and attached himself to one of the citizens of that country, and he sent him into his fields to feed swine. And he was longing to fill his stomach with the pods that the swine were eating, and*

no one was giving anything to him. But when he came to his senses, he said, 'How many of my father's hired men have more than enough bread, but I am dying here with hunger! I will get up and go to my father and will say to him, "Father, I have sinned against heaven, and in your sight; I am no longer worthy to be called your son; make me as one of your hired men."' And he got up and came to his father. But while he was still a long way off, his father saw him, and felt compassion for him, and ran and embraced him, and kissed him. And the son said to him, 'Father, I have sinned against heaven and in your sight; I am no longer worthy to be called your son.' But the father said to his slaves, 'Quickly bring out the best robe and put it on him, and put a ring on his hand and sandals on his feet; and bring the fattened calf, kill it, and let us eat and be merry; for this son of mine was dead, and has come to life again; he was lost, and has been found.' And they began to be merry."

The son in this parable is like many sons today—foolish, greedy, self-centered, overly indulgent, eager to get his hands on wealth he has not earned, and wasteful in the way he spends money in the company of irresponsible, uncaring people who leave him in misery when the resources are gone. As he comes to his senses in a pigsty, his condition mirrors his life. Realizing that his father's servants have it much better than he does, he resolves to go back home.

The last thing the son expects is to be forgiven. He just wants the opportunity to return home, acknowledge what a terrible, derelict son he's been, and become a slave. At least then he would have a place to live and decent food to eat.

In describing the son's arrival at his father's house, Jesus teaches us what it means to forgive, based on how God forgives. As soon as the father sees the son from a distance, he runs to meet him, lovingly and wholeheartedly embraces his son, and orders an extravagant celebration to mark his return. That illustrates the lavish character of God's forgiveness. When He sees the sinner moving in His direction with a repentant heart and a readiness to confess his sins, God embraces him and immediately showers His forgiving love on that sinner.

The father in the parable is nothing like people in the church who carry the ungodly and unscriptural attitude of bitterness. Such people, who think they have to retaliate for every wrong committed against them and react to preserve their pride, are so unlike the character of Jesus Christ.

Bitter people are not willing to forgive, and their grudge-filled actions undermine the church's work and the life and ministry of faithful servants and leaders. What a contrast to the father who rejoices over the repentant son and spares no expense to express his forgiveness. And the father does none of this for personal gain, but simply for the sheer joy of reconciliation. The parable pictures God's way of forgiveness, which is why we can say again that forgiveness is the most godlike action anyone can perform (cf. Matt. 5:43-45).

Forgiveness is also the apostle Paul's salient point in Ephesians 4:32: "And be kind to one another, tender-hearted, forgiving each other, just as God in Christ also has forgiven you." A forgiving attitude is the key ingredient in treating others kindly and tenderly. We have already seen that God loves us and forgives us, not because we are so deserving, but purely because He is so overwhelmingly gracious. Therefore, in the same way believers should—in the midst of an extremely angry, merciless, unkind world—extend simple kindness and tenderheartedness to other believers, forgiving sins, failures, and weaknesses and disregarding their own selfish agendas and personal expectations.

In Colossians 3:13 Paul reveals another salient truth about Christian forgiveness: "bearing with one another, and forgiving each other, whoever has a complaint against any one; just as the Lord forgave you, so also should you." We are to forgive with the same kind of magnanimity and generosity that God forgave us.

THE IMPERATIVE OF FORGIVENESS

Another of Jesus' parables that vividly drives home the importance of forgiveness in the Christian life is the Parable of the Unforgiving Servant. In this passage Jesus' teaching underscores not only the necessity of forgiveness but also the imperative that if God, who has received the greater offense, can forgive us, then believers, who have been offended far less, must forgive fellow believers.

In response to Peter's question concerning how often a believer should forgive the sins of a brother, our Lord related the following parable to all the disciples:

> *"For this reason the kingdom of heaven may be compared to a certain king who wished to settle accounts with his slaves. And when he had begun to settle them, there was brought to him one who owed him ten thousand talents. But since he did not have the means to repay, his lord commanded him to be sold, along with his wife and children and all that he had, and repayment to be made. The slave therefore falling down, prostrated himself before him, saying, 'Have patience with me, and I will repay you everything.' And the lord of that slave felt compassion and released him and forgave him the debt. But that slave went out and found one of his fellow-slaves who owed him a hundred denarii; and he seized him and began to choke him, saying, 'Pay back what you owe.' So his fellow-slave fell down and began to entreat him, saying 'Have patience with me and I will repay you.' He was unwilling however, but went and threw him in prison until he should pay back what was owed. So when his fellow-slaves saw what had happened, they were deeply grieved and came and reported to their lord all that had happened. Then summoning him, his lord said to him, 'You wicked slave, I forgave you all that debt because you entreated me. Should you not also have had mercy on your fellow-slave, even as I had mercy on you?' And his lord, moved with anger, handed him over to the torturers until he should repay all that was owed him. So shall My heavenly Father also do to you, if each of you does not forgive his brother from your heart."*
>
> *—Matt. 18:23-35*

In ancient kingdoms all citizens were slaves in the broad sense that they were subjects of the monarch. That means noblemen were as much the ruler's slaves as were low-ranking servants. This parable suggests such extremes, which indicates its truth applies to every believer in God's kingdom. The first slave in the parable had a lot of personal wealth, but the second slave was probably poor by comparison. The first man was likely a governor in the kingdom, and it was his primary responsibility to collect taxes for the king.

The parable's point regarding the money is that the servant owed an extremely large, unpayable debt to the king. That tremendous debt symbolizes the enormous debt of sin that every human being owes to God. When God's Spirit convicts an individual of his or her sin (John 16:8), he or she realizes that sin's debt is beyond comprehension and is humanly unpayable (cf. Job 42:6; Ezra 9:6: Rom. 7:13).

God wants us to see life as a stewardship that is to be lived for His glory. But unbelievers take the life they've been given by God and squander it on themselves rather than investing it for Him. Like the prodigal son or the servant who buried his talent, they waste whatever gospel privilege the Lord grants them.

The first slave in the parable represents the unbeliever who has been given life by God (Acts 17:25), has the opportunity to give God what He is owed (cf. Rom. 11:36), but wastes God's resources in sin. Indicative of any bankrupt sinner, the man probably embezzled what rightfully belonged to the king and consumed it all on his own desires. That resulted in the slave's punishment when "his lord commanded him to be sold, along with his wife and children and all that he had, and repayment to be made" (Matt. 18:25).

When confronted with his sin and its consequences, the slave prostrated himself before the king, signifying his complete submission to the ruler's mercy. The man was thoroughly convicted by his sin and was genuinely penitent. Every sinner should be as overcome by his sin as that slave was by his debt (see Matt. 5:3-12; Luke 18:13).

Even though the likelihood of making things right was virtually nonexistent, the man in his desperation pleaded for an opportunity to do so: "Have patience with me, and I will repay you everything" (Matt. 18:26). The king's subsequent gesture of forbearing kindness pictures God's great forgiving love for the truly repentant sinner who knows he must rely on the Lord's mercy. He releases the sinner from the impossible debt of sin and declares him a new person in Christ. (Obviously, the gospel message is implied, not completely outlined, in this parable, because the main point Jesus wanted to illustrate is the subject of forgiveness between believers.)

The attitude and behavior of the forgiven slave toward one of his fellow slaves, in the second part of the parable, is truly unbelievable and unacceptable in the wake of the king's magnanimous gesture. Even though the second slave's debt was infinitely smaller than the first slave's, the newly pardoned servant was totally unwilling to emulate the king and forgive the other servant. It's not that the second man's debt to the first man was not legitimate. It was real and did need forgiveness, which the first man refused to extend. Instead, he acted in a proud, presumptuous, ungrateful, and unmerciful fashion toward the lower-ranking slave.

That the forgiven slave would demand repayment from the other slave, and do so in an angry, abusive manner, was grossly insensitive, irrational, and, in the words of one commentator, a "moral monstrosity." And the unforgiving slave was punished for this sin when other slaves (representing other believers) were rightly grieved and reported the incident to the king.

The monarch, even as our holy and just God would be, was "moved with anger" (v. 34) at the man's unthinkable sin. The worst aspect of the sin was not the demand for repayment of a relatively small debt, but the stubborn refusal to forgive a fellow servant in the spirit in which the first servant had found mercy. The forgiven servant was definitely not following the principle later expressed by the apostle Paul in Ephesians 4:32.

When God does need to chasten believers for any grievous sin, it is perfectly evenhanded, more so than any king's punishment could be. The Lord, while always angry at sin, disciplines his own because He loves them (Heb. 12:6, 10-11). If they forget the forgiveness they've received (as the first slave did) and refuse to forgive fellow believers, God causes them to endure such "torturers" as stress, hardships, troubled consciences, and other trials until they deal with the sin. James says: "Judgment will be merciless to one who has shown no mercy" (Jas. 2:13).

I believe the lesson of the parable is clear: any believer who offends a fellow believer has offended God much more, and God has forgiven him; therefore, the offended believer should always be willing to forgive the brother or sister who sins against him or her and asks to be forgiven. Christians must always reflect God's forgiveness because they have experienced that same forgiveness.

Genuine forgiveness, however, does not excuse the wrongs of others. Compassion and mercy will not rationalize an offense away but will always call it what it is. But in confronting a sin, the forgiving believer will eliminate bitterness and all other negative feelings that can only increase the sin rather than eliminate it. Then he or she can confidently and sincerely pray the familiar prayer, "Forgive us our debts, as we also have forgiven our debtors" (Matt. 6:12).

THE BLESSINGS OF FORGIVENESS

"Blessed are the merciful," our Lord said, "for they shall receive mercy" (Matt. 5:7). If we want to enjoy the benefits of God's forgiveness toward us, we must be willing to forgive other believers, even those who repeatedly sin against us. Or we can express this final principle more directly, which is that God does not forgive those who do not forgive others (Matt. 6:15).

That does not mean that an unforgiving attitude nullifies a believer's salvation. In the eternal scope of things, God forgives all the sins of those who are in Jesus Christ. But an attitude that refuses to forgive fellow believers will rob a Christian of his joy, peace, fellowship, and usefulness in the church. This is the principle John 13:9-10 refers to: "Simon Peter said to Him, 'Lord, not my feet only, but also my hands and my head.' Jesus said to him, 'He who has bathed needs only to wash his feet, but is completely clean; and you are clean.'" It's not a question of being clean, or saved, but of removing the dirt of ongoing sin so that we may have proper fellowship.

If we are justified we possess eternal forgiveness, and that settles the issue of future blessing. But temporal forgiveness, given and received, is a necessary part of our sanctification process and determines whether or not we will have present blessing. If we don't forgive other believers regularly and consistently, God won't extend temporal forgiveness to us. As a result, we will forfeit our current blessing and suffer divine chastening. As we saw in the Parable of the Unforgiving Servant in Matthew 18, God chastens believers who do not forgive other believers, sometimes even to the point of death.

In my many years of pastoral experience I've found that Christians who lack joy, power, and usefulness in their walk often express an unforgiving attitude. God withholds blessing because of their bitter, grudge-filled, stubborn spirit.

I've had unforgiving people seek counsel from me and express their anger, frustration, and confusion at the difficulties they were experiencing. In those cases I generally ask them these questions: What do you think the Lord is trying to do in your life? Could there be some reason you're experiencing all this trouble? The point of my questions is that these people need to examine their hearts, because that's the source of their anger and bitterness. I challenge them to see if their unforgiving attitudes are causing their chastening. I remind them that believers must forgive because that's when they most reflect the heart of their heavenly Father.

In Matthew 5:23-24 Jesus teaches, "If therefore you are presenting your offering at the altar, and there remember that your brother has something against you, leave your offering there before the altar, and go your way; first be reconciled to your brother, and then come and present your offering."

The meaning of our Lord's teaching couldn't be clearer. An unsettled grudge needs to be resolved and reconciliation must occur before we can render true worship to God. We must do all we can to settle any anger, bitterness, and unforgivingness we hold toward a brother or sister in Christ, or that he or she holds toward us. Otherwise, we are not fit to come before God or partake of His

Communion table. That's why the attitude of forgiveness is so critical in the life of the church.

To help guard your hearts against the tendency to not forgive other believers, remember this prayer:

O God, give me a heart of forgiveness, so that I may commune with You in the fullness of fellowship and joy and not experience the chastening that comes when You don't forgive me because I won't forgive a brother or sister in Christ. May I remember that for everyone who sins against me I have sinned multiplied times against You, and You have always forgiven me. At no time has any of my sin caused me to forfeit my eternal life; therefore, no one else's sin should cause them to forfeit my love and my mercy toward them. Amen.

8

REASON ENOUGH
TO REJOICE

Every individual has a basic desire for joy, and it seems that all other desires flow from there and directly or indirectly serve that most basic need. People consume certain foods and beverages because they get enjoyment from them. People seek to gain money and material possessions because they believe those things will bring joy. Most people seek prestige, power, and success because they think those will also bring joy. But that kind of enjoyment is temporary and disappointing. Real and lasting joy comes only as believers, by faith through grace, trust Jesus Christ as Lord and Savior and appropriate the truths of His kingdom.

The nature of true joy comes into perspective when we contrast the definitions of the word. Its primary meaning, according to Webster's dictionary, is "an emotion evoked by well-being, success, or good fortune or by the prospect of possessing what one desires." Implicit in that definition are all the man-centered, temporal, ultimately unsatisfying gratifications we just referred to.

Now consider the scriptural definition of joy. The Greek term (*chara*) is used approximately seventy times in the New Testament, and it always represents a feeling of happiness that is based on spiritual realities. Joy in those contexts is not merely something experienced as a result of favorable circumstances. It is not even merely a divinely stimulated human emotion. Rather, joy is a supernatural gift from God to believers. That is what Nehemiah was referring to when he said, "The joy of the LORD is your strength" (Neh. 8:10).

Scriptural joy is not only a gift from God, it is also commanded of all those who know Him: "Rejoice in the Lord always; again I will say, rejoice!" (Phil. 4:4; cf. 1 Thess. 5:16). Like other vital characteristics of the Christian life (being filled with the Holy Spirit, realizing our spiritual unity, etc.), believers don't need to manufacture joy or utilize all kinds of gimmicks to find it. They simply need to thank the Lord for the gift and revel in the wonderful blessings joy already affords (see Rom. 14:17).

JOY: A REPEATED COMMAND

Because God commands believers to have joy, it easily follows that joy is another foundational pillar or attitude of Christian character. The evil world in which we live offers us plenty of reasons to be anxious, disturbed, worried, and fearful, but none of those negative factors ought to seriously affect the believer. That's because the New Testament is replete with exhortations and instructions about joy. Philippians alone mentions it seventeen times. We've already noted the apostle Paul's basic command in 4:4, but he also talks about joy in these key verses (emphases added):

I know that I shall remain and continue with you all for your progress and joy *in the faith.*

—1:25

Make my joy *complete by being of the same mind.*

—2:2

But even if I am being poured out as a drink offering upon the sacrifice and service of your faith, I rejoice *and share my* joy *with you all. And you too, I urge you,* rejoice *in the same way and share your* joy *with me.*

—2:17-18

Finally, my brethren, rejoice *in the Lord.*

—*3:1*

But I rejoiced *in the Lord greatly.*

—*4:10*

In light of such an emphasis on joy, it is safe to assert that no circumstance or event should ever diminish the joy in a believer's life. That may sound ridiculous or impossible, especially given the realities of daily life. But it's based on the truth of Scripture. First Thessalonians 5:16 is most concise, direct, and inescapable: "Rejoice always." And Paul himself practiced this command, acknowledging that although he faced many hardships, he was always rejoicing (2 Cor. 6:10). The apostle Peter's words also affirm this premise: "But to the degree that you share the sufferings of Christ, keep on rejoicing; so that also at the revelation of His glory, you may rejoice with exultation" (1 Pet. 4:13).

Many other New Testament texts reinforce the truth that no amount of adversity or difficulty should affect a believer's joyful attitude. The Lord Jesus Himself underscored the importance of joy when he taught the disciples in the Upper Room, just prior to His own sufferings and death. Joy was an essential component of the legacy He left us (emphases added):

> *"These things I have spoken to you, that My* joy *may be in you, and that your* joy *may be made full."*
> —*John 15:11*

> *"Therefore you, too, now have sorrow; but I will see you again, and your heart will* rejoice, *and no one takes your* joy *away from you."*
> —*John 16:22*

> *"Until now you have asked for nothing in My name; ask, and you will receive, that your* joy *may be made full."*
> —*John 16:24*

"But now I come to Thee; and these things I speak in the world, that they may have My joy made full in themselves."
                                                                —John 17:13

If you read the entire context of John 13—17, you'll see that in the midst of the frightening circumstances of the Lord's impending death, the Twelve would soon be left in the world to face persecution, suffering, and eventually death. Yet the Lord never wavered from telling them they would constantly have joy.

Jesus' words in His Upper Room message, however, should not surprise us, because early in His ministry He taught that trials and adversity need not diminish the believer's sense of joy. Matthew 5:11-12 says, "Blessed are you when men revile you, and persecute you, and say all kinds of evil against you falsely, on account of Me. Rejoice, and be glad, for your reward in heaven is great, for so they persecuted the prophets who were before you." Luke records much the same message: "Blessed are you when men hate you, and ostracize you, and heap insults upon you, and spurn your name as evil, for the sake of the Son of Man. Be glad in that day, and leap for joy, for behold, your reward is great in heaven; for in the same way their fathers used to treat the prophets" (Luke 6:22-23).

But that still leaves unanswered the question, how is it possible to respond to every difficult situation with rejoicing? The apostle James is instructive at this point when he says, "Consider it all joy, my brethren, when you encounter various trials, knowing that the testing of your faith produces endurance" (Jas. 1:2-3).

We ought to be happier about our times of trial than our good times because the trials are always more spiritually productive and refining. They are much more likely to strip away our self-centeredness and pride and convince us we are not in control of everything. We become much more dependent on the Lord during times of testing, and that enhances our prayer lives and makes us much more sympathetic toward Christ's sufferings and everyone else's as well. James calls these kinds of effects the "perfect result" of endurance, which makes us "perfect [mature] and complete, lacking in nothing" (1:4).

The call to rejoice at all times and in all circumstances does not mean, however, that there are not times when it's all right to refrain from outward expressions of joy. It is legitimate for us at appropriate times to identify with normal human emotions, just as Paul encourages us in Romans 12:15: "Rejoice with those who rejoice, and weep with those who weep." There is something good and beneficial for us and those we minister to when we legitimately shed tears and show compassion to those dealing with pain and sorrow. However, that shouldn't disrupt or diminish the Christian's internal, abiding sense of joy.

Paul expresses the proper balance when he says, "As sorrowful yet always rejoicing" (2 Cor. 6:10). There is a place for normal human sympathy and grief, but it should always be accompanied by a heart that is rejoicing. Underneath the outward emotions of weeping and sadness and the gestures of sympathy, the believer will always have genuine spiritual rejoicing, an attitude only God can give.

THE SUPERIORITY OF TRUE JOY

As we stated at the beginning of this chapter, the world's joy is inferior to the true joy God so graciously gives believers and commands them to express. Quite simply, the world's joy is derived from fleeting earthly pleasures. Scripture is careful to identify worldly joy and warn of its dangers and inadequacies.

The Inferiority of the World's Joy

The writer of Ecclesiastes tells of his own folly in being caught up in earthly joy: "And all that my eyes desired I did not refuse them. I did not withhold my heart from any pleasure, for my heart was pleased because of all my labor and this was my reward for all my labor. Thus I considered all my activities which my hands had done and the labor which I had exerted, and behold all was vanity [futility] and striving after wind and there was no profit under the sun" (Eccles. 2:10-11). Then in Ecclesiastes 11:9 the Preacher declares God's displeasure with such self-indulgences: "Rejoice, young man, during your childhood, and let your heart be pleasant during the days of young manhood. And follow the impulses of your heart and the desires of your eyes. Yet know that God will bring you to judgment for all these things" (cf. 7:6; Isa. 16:10; Jas. 4:9).

Along the way to that judgment, worldly joy can be very deceptive and deluding: "There is a way which seems right to a man, but its end is the way of death. Even in laughter the heart may be in pain, and the end of joy may be grief" (Prov. 14:12-13). People constantly want things, and they impulsively rush to fulfill those desires only to discover that their joy soon turns to grief. Earthly joy doesn't last beyond such short-term pleasures. That's why Job 20:4-5 asks this pointed question: "Do you know this from of old, from the establishment of man on earth, that the triumphing of the wicked is short, and the joy of the godless momentary?"

Thankfulness in the Midst of True Joy

In contrast to earthly joy, true spiritual joy for the believer is supernatural. Biblical joy is far superior to worldly joy and any of its psychological and materialistic explanations. The apostle Paul in Galatians 5:22 identifies joy as an aspect of the fruit of the Spirit. In Romans 14:17 he further defines joy as an essential component of the kingdom of God; it's a spiritual joy that comes from God through Jesus Christ, dispensed by the Holy Spirit. And no circumstance in life, other than when we sin, should legitimately take away our joy if we truly know and trust the Lord. Even when sin does rob us of joy, that experience should not last long because as soon as we confess our sin, God allows us to rejoice in His forgiveness (1 John 1:9).

Because true joy gives us confidence that God is sovereignly unfolding everything for our good and His glory, we have abundant reason to rejoice and thank the Lord for what He is doing in our lives. The following are just some of the reasons we who know Christ ought to constantly be joyful.

First, we ought to have joy because *joy is an act of proper response to the character of God*. Joy originates because we know God is sovereign, gracious, loving, merciful, kind, omnipotent, omniscient, and omnipresent. Because He seeks our well-being, we can have confidence in the midst of everything He brings our way. That's based on a deep, heartfelt knowledge of God that realizes that when people mean things for evil, He means them for our good (Gen. 50:20). We are confident that He works all things together for good to those who love Him (Rom. 8:28). We can't always rejoice in our circumstances alone, but we can always rejoice in the God who controls our circumstances.

Our joy in God's character is further enhanced because His character is unchanging. It would indeed be frightening if God were capricious and we could never rely on His words and actions. But God is not like that. His grace is always consistently dispensed. His justice is always righteous and fair. He always fulfills what He promises. James 1:17 assures us of these truths: "Every good thing bestowed and every perfect gift is from above, coming down from the Father of lights, with whom there is no variation, or shifting shadow."

Second, Christians should rejoice because *joy is a proper response to the work of Christ*. As we remember that "while we were yet sinners, Christ died for us" (Rom. 5:8), we should immediately praise and thank Him with joyful hearts. It is important to remember that we "were not redeemed with perishable things like silver or gold from [our] futile way of life inherited from [our] forefathers, but with precious blood, as of a lamb unblemished and spotless, the blood of Christ" (1 Pet. 1:18-19), that "He Himself bore our sins in His body on the cross, that we might die to sin and live to righteousness; for by His wounds you were healed" (2:24), that "the blood of Jesus His Son cleanses us from all sin" (1 John 1:7), and that God orchestrated it all "before the foundation of the world, that we should be holy and blameless before Him. In love He predestined us to adoption as sons through Jesus Christ to Himself, according to the kind intention of His will" (Eph. 1:4-5). When we understand all that Christ has accomplished for us and that heaven is eternally ours, we have an abiding joy that no trivial, passing circumstance should affect.

Third, we ought to have incessant spiritual joy as *a show of confidence in the work of the Holy Spirit*. In addition to giving us the gift of joy itself (Rom. 14:17; Gal. 5:22), the Spirit is continually, ever increasingly showing us the things of Christ and making us more like the Savior: "But we all, with unveiled face beholding as in a mirror the glory of the Lord, are being transformed into the same image from glory to glory, just as from the Lord, the Spirit" (2 Cor. 3:18). In our own strength and wisdom we cannot know the mind of God, but the Spirit who lives in us (Rom. 8:9-10) helps us understand spiritual things (1 Cor. 2:10-16). The Holy Spirit leads us into all truth (John 16:13) and teaches us and reminds us of all that we need to know in the Christian life (John 14:26). The Spirit is the down payment, the first installment of our eternal inheritance (Eph. 1:13-14). And we have the confidence that every day He is interceding before the throne of grace on our behalf (Rom. 8:26-27).

Fourth, we should have joy because it is *a reasonable response to continual spiritual blessings*. God's pouring out of spiritual blessings for believers never stops, as Ephesians 1:3 indicates: "Blessed be the God and Father of our Lord Jesus Christ, who has blessed us with every spiritual blessing in the heavenly places in Christ."

We may not always feel that our lives are especially blessed from day to day, but if we just pause and consider some of the ways the Lord is good to us, we will not be able to keep from rejoicing. For example, every time we sin it is instantly forgiven. Every time God refines us through trials, exposes us to solid biblical teaching, and molds us more toward the image of Christ, it should be cause for us to praise Him. Every time God brings us safely through another day and spares us some terrible disaster or extreme agony, we experience the blessing of His mercy. God is also planning future blessings, such as preparing a place for us in heaven (John 14:2-3).

All the endless favors, seen and unseen, that God does for us throughout life are evidences that His children are abundantly blessed. And those blessings mean we should express true spiritual joy every day and never take them for granted or question their benefits in helping us grow.

A fifth reason to manifest joy is that it's *a proper response to God's providence*. Divine providence is simply the way God orchestrates all circumstances to effect the greatest good for believers. It is by far the most common method He uses to arrange and control temporal human events. When we consider God's drawing together of millions of details and situations to accomplish His perfect purpose, the vast scope of providence is a much greater miracle than those one-time supernatural occurrences we usually call miracles.

What a settled confidence and deep-down assurance is ours in knowing that the Lord, through all the infinite contingencies, sovereignly controls the entire universe. Furthermore, He also graciously controls all the specific events in our individual lives, which should continually renew our faith and joy in Him.

Sixth, Christians should have joy because it's *a proper response to the promise of future glory.* As I indicated in the Introduction to my book *The Glory of Heaven* (Wheaton, Ill.: Crossway Books, 1996), believers today are not captivated enough with the joyful prospect that one day they will enter heaven and dwell in its glories for all eternity. We become so comfortable with the temporary joys of this life, or so mired down with its difficulties, that we forget we are merely pilgrims "looking for the city [heaven] which has foundations, whose architect and builder is God" (Heb. 11:10; cf. 13:14).

Once we get into the habit of dwelling frequently on the glories of what is to come, the problems and struggles of life—even the mundane daily affairs—all fade into insignificance by comparison (cf. Rom. 8:18). When the apostle Paul tells us to "set your mind on the things above, not on the things that are on earth" (Col. 3:2), he intends it to be a joyful exercise that frees our minds from all the debilitating stuff of earth—things that don't matter for eternity anyway. Such temporal concerns ought never to dampen our spiritual joy.

During the time my sister was suffering from terminal cancer (she passed away in 1997 and now knows the joys of heaven firsthand), we spoke to each other frequently by telephone. During one of those calls several years ago, I said to her, "Well, Julie, the worst thing that could happen to you is the best thing that could happen to anybody."

She answered, "I know that; I've never questioned it."

Then I added, "You know, you're going to be in the presence of the Lord, in the glories of heaven."

To which she replied, "And that's my confidence."

Then she told me how the hospital that day had sent a psychiatrist and someone else to tell her they wanted to place her in a special therapy group. They hoped to help her get in touch with her "inner child."

My sister reacted to that idea by telling the hospital personnel, "No thanks. I don't need to get in touch with my inner child. I'm in touch with my Lord Jesus Christ, and everything is fine."

We can face any situation with that kind of hope in our hearts. We simply should not get too disturbed about anything that happens to us on earth because it is all so temporary. The events of this life just make heaven all the more alluring and wonderful.

A seventh reason we must have joy is because *it demonstrates thankfulness for answered prayer*. Jesus said, "Ask, and you will receive, that your joy may be made full" (John 16:24). The Lord has always answered our requests and intercessions in ways that were completely consistent with His will (1 John 5:14-15). He has done that countless times so that for all our answered prayers—and for all those yet unanswered—our joy should be undiminished.

Furthermore, true joy demonstrates *a genuine thankfulness and appreciation for God's Word*. At the end of Chapter 6 we discussed how valuable Scripture is for our spiritual growth. That truth ought to keep us from ever abandoning our attitude of rejoicing before the Lord. His goodness and mercy in giving us the Word should make us echo David's words, "The precepts of the LORD are right, rejoicing the heart" (Ps. 19:8; cf. 119:14, 24, 70, 97, 103, 111, 127, 140, 162). The prophet Jeremiah expressed similar sentiments, which should further encourage our thanks for God's truth: "Thy words were found and I ate them, and Thy words became for me a joy and the delight of my heart; for I have been called by Thy name, O LORD God of hosts" (Jer. 15:16).

The New Testament also testifies to the joy that must be ours in response to God's Word. The apostle John, in the introduction to his first letter, says, "These things we write to you that your joy may be full" (1 John 1:4, NKJV). He knew that Scripture would elicit the deepest appreciation and joy in its readers as they thank the Lord for everything He has given them.

Finally, *appreciation for Christian fellowship* should always cause us to rejoice. Paul told the Thessalonians, "For what thanks can we render to God for you in return for all the joy with which we rejoice before our God on your account" (1 Thess. 3:9).

WHAT IF JOY IS LACKING?

In spite of all the scriptural reasons for obeying God's command to sincerely rejoice at all times, all believers will experience times when joy will be lacking in their lives. Paul commands all believers to "Test yourselves to see if you are in the faith; examine yourselves!" (2 Cor. 13:5). If joy is absent from your life, there are a number of tests you can apply to discover the reason.

First, it could be that *you don't know the Lord*. You might be relying on a false assurance of salvation. This is what Jesus told the disciples as He interpreted His parable of the soils: "And the one on whom seed was sown on the rocky places, this is the man who hears the word, and immediately receives it with joy; yet he has no firm root in himself, but is only temporary, and when affliction or persecution arises because of the word, immediately he falls away" (Matt. 13:20-21; cf. vv. 5-6). Sometimes when people first hear the Gospel there is an immediate sense of emotional joy and a psychological lift, but it doesn't last. If a person constantly struggles to have joy and is unable to get on top of life's challenges, it may mean he doesn't really know Christ. If so, he needs to heed Paul's command in 2 Corinthians 13:5 and repent and believe.

Second, you might lack joy because *you are under some very strong temptation*. The apostle Peter writes, "Be of sober spirit, be on the alert. Your adversary, the devil, prowls about like a roaring lion, seeking someone to devour" (1 Pet. 5:8). Satan enjoys nothing more than being able to steal your joy during times of severe temptation. The solution is, do not allow your worries to become temptations: "casting all your anxiety upon Him, because He cares for you" (1 Pet. 5:7).

Sometimes you have no joy because *you entertain false and unreal-istic expectations*. Christians often believe they deserve more blessings than they have, when in reality they already have far more than they deserve. Before we came to Christ we deserved—like all unregen-erate sinners—God's wrath and an eternity in hell. "But God demonstrates His own love toward us, in that while we were yet sin-ners, Christ died for us. Much more then, having now been justi-fied by His blood, we shall be saved from the wrath of God through Him" (Rom. 5:8-9). We who deserved nothing have all the more rea-son to rejoice and be grateful for the many blessings the Lord bestows.

False expectations are directly related to pride, and *the sin of pride* is another common reason you may not experience joy. More specif-ically, I'm referring to the ugly sin of dissatisfaction with your pos-sessions. Western culture, with its emphasis on materialism and greed, encourages that mentality. Glamorous models appear in tele-vision commercials and make you unhappy with your own image or that of your spouse. Advertisers promote their cars, electronics, vaca-tions, and household goods in an attempt to make you dissatisfied with what you currently have—or don't have.

Our pride, if unchecked, can cause us to give in to those worldly influences. It will then prompt us to chase after temporal things, and we end up relinquishing our joy and contentment for frustration and dissatisfaction.

Prayerlessness can also steal your joy. If you fail to heed 1 Peter 5:7 when faced with trials and difficulties, it's certain that you'll forfeit the sense of joy God wants you to have. You simply don't need to carry the entire burden yourself: "Be anxious for nothing, but in everything by prayer and supplication with thanksgiving let your requests be made known to God. And the peace of God, which sur-passes all comprehension, shall guard your hearts and your minds in Christ Jesus" (Phil. 4:6-7).

Joseph Scriven, in the first stanza of his familiar hymn "What a Friend We Have in Jesus," aptly expresses the importance of prayer and underscores what happens when it is lacking:

What a Friend we have in Jesus, all our sins and griefs to bear!
What a privilege to carry everything to God in prayer!
O what peace we often forfeit, O what needless pain we bear,
All because we do not carry everything to God in prayer.

Finally, the main contributor to lack of joy is *ignorance*. If you are truly growing in Christ, you will have true spiritual joy. If, on the other hand, you live on impulse and subjective feelings, you will have great difficulty sustaining joy. It's imperative that you control your emotions, and that can happen only when you fill your mind with sound doctrine, believe it wholeheartedly, and walk by the Holy Spirit.

The world loves to operate on the basis of what feels good. But the Lord has a far superior standard for believers, as the apostle Paul indicates: "Do not be conformed to this world, but be transformed by the renewing of your mind, that you may prove what the will of God is, that which is good and acceptable and perfect" (Rom. 12:2). When that is true, we will respond joyfully and intelligently to all that God has for us.

If our minds are fully and consistently informed by God's truth, and if we adopt one small but significant habit of the early church, we would undoubtedly be more aware of the importance of joy. The regular greeting between individual believers in the early church was the Greek *Chairete*, which literally means "rejoice." Jesus originated this greeting the morning of the Resurrection, when He met some of the women who had just heard of His rising from the dead: "As they went to tell His disciples, behold, Jesus met them, saying, 'Rejoice!' So they came and held Him by the feet and worshiped Him" (Matt. 28:9, NKJV). That was certainly the appropriate greeting as our Lord sought to comfort and encourage His followers by His presence, which was clear and irrefutable evidence of His resurrection.

"Rejoice," which among believers is a much more meaningful salutation than the routine "Hi" or "Good morning," became the early Christians' common form of greeting. They realized joy was a command, and there was always reason for them to rejoice as the church expanded and matured. With all the riches that are ours in Christ, we also have every reason to rejoice. Perhaps our own regular use of the greeting "Rejoice" would remind us more often of the scriptural injunction that our joy is to be great and always evident.

ALWAYS A PLACE
FOR GRATITUDE

Ingratitude is one of the ugliest attitudes anyone can possess. The Gospel of Luke drives home this point in a fascinating passage that has been vividly etched in my mind ever since I first read it many years ago. It's the story of the ten lepers:

> *And it came about while He was on the way to Jerusalem, that He was passing between Samaria and Galilee. And as He entered a certain village, there met Him ten leprous men, who stood at a distance; and they raised their voices saying, "Jesus, Master, have mercy on us!" And when He saw them, He said to them, "Go and show yourselves to the priests." And it came about that as they were going, they were cleansed. Now one of them, when he saw that he had been healed, turned back, glorifying God with a loud voice, and he fell on his face at His feet, giving thanks to Him. And he was a Samaritan. And Jesus answered and said, "Were there not ten cleansed? But the nine—where are they? Were none found who turned back to give glory to God, except this foreigner?" And He said to him, "Rise, and go your way; your faith has made you well."*
>
> *—17:11-19*

In those days lepers were quarantined in colonies, some distance away from cities and towns because their dreaded disease was so contagious. That's why in Luke's account the group of ten stood some distance away as Jesus and the others entered the village.

Jesus' seemingly strange command for the men to show themselves to the priest was part of the normal process, as prescribed in the Law of Moses, for dealing with leprosy and aiding with recovery from it. When a person was confident that he or she was recovered from the disease, he or she was to submit to a purification ceremony from the priest to ensure—as much as was possible in ancient times—that he or she was indeed healed and could rejoin normal society. In this remarkable account, the healing occurred miraculously and unmistakably as the men exercised faith and went to see the priest.

It is almost inconceivable that anyone could be cured from a frightening disease such as leprosy, which isolated a man or woman from family and friends and cut him or her off from normal events in society and the synagogue, and not be abundantly and permanently grateful. But that is exactly what happened with nine out of the ten lepers Jesus healed. Furthermore, the grateful one was a Samaritan, which meant he was from the half-breed ethnic group that was the product of Jewish intermarriage with the Canaanites and the Assyrians. Samaritans were despised by devout Jews, and as a result a mutual hatred had developed between the two peoples. So it was indeed remarkable that a Samaritan should be the only one falling on his face at the feet of Jesus, a Jew, and thanking Him.

The story of the ten lepers is a powerful illustration of just how ugly the sin of ingratitude is. But the attitude of thanklessness displayed by the nine lepers is not so unexpected from those who have no saving relationship to Christ. In the apostle Paul's indictment of unbelieving humanity and its sinful society in Romans 1:18-32, his accusation is very specific. Verse 21 begins with the phrase, "for even though they knew God," which means everyone coming into the world knows about God, even though they don't have a personal, saving faith in Him. But then Paul says, "They did not honor Him as God, or *give thanks*" (emphasis added). The thankless person despises the very notion of grace, the undeserved goodness granted by God.

Thus ingratitude is a sin that characterizes the unregenerate, and it appears right at the top of God's list of damning sins in Romans 1.

Paul later reinforced this truth when he told Timothy, "But realize this, that in the last days difficult times will come. For men will be lovers of self, lovers of money, boastful, arrogant, revilers, disobedient to parents, *ungrateful*, unholy" (2 Tim. 3:1-2, emphasis added). In the end-times, ingratitude will still characterize people—even more so than currently. As we get closer to the return of Christ, people will become more wicked and less grateful. For example, the contemporary unregenerate person seems to be constantly bitter or complaining about his circumstances, hoping for some "lucky break" to change his lot in life. Or he might reluctantly and fatalistically accept whatever comes along, claiming that he can't change things anyway. Or he might egotistically thank himself for who he is and what he has, thinking that everything in his life results solely from his own efforts. No matter how they're manifested, ingratitude or the absence of gratitude have always been traits God hates. Therefore believers must continually strive to be thankful in all circumstances.

THE COMMAND TO BE THANKFUL

As Christians, we can understand that the nine lepers who didn't know Christ as Lord and Savior would be thankless and that the unsaved culture around us is characterized by ingratitude. However, it is virtually impossible to understand or accept an ungrateful believer when we consider all that the Lord has done for His own. In fact, just as we saw in the previous chapter on joy, an attitude of thankfulness is impossible for believers to ignore because God's Word commands it: "In everything give thanks; for this is God's will for you in Christ Jesus" (1 Thess. 5:18).

The precedent for that command was established in the Old Testament. The thank offerings or peace offerings (Lev. 3:1-17; 7:11-36) were designed to remind God's people of their need to be thankful to Him. They would bring to Him a sheaf of grain and some oil and wine as thank offerings. These were symbols of all the Lord's provision and tangible reminders that believers need to thank Him regularly for His grace and mercy in supplying all they have. The church today has an ordinance that serves the same purpose. At Communion, or the Lord's Table, we combine elements of the thank offering as well as elements of the sin offering as we thank God for all that Christ's death accomplished. When we observe this ordinance we are essentially presenting a thank offering.

The apostle Paul's command in 1 Thessalonians 5:18 to be grateful in everything means that for the believer gratitude should be connected to everything that occurs in his or her life, no matter how pleasant or difficult it is. And, as with joy, the only thing that will legitimately dampen our attitude of thanksgiving is unconfessed sin. No matter what the situation or trial, there is always reason to thank the Lord.

If we truly know God, we know that He is unfolding His agenda and purpose in our lives. He has sovereignly determined each part of His plan for us so that we'll be benefited and He'll be glorified (cf. Rom. 8:28). We should not be surprised or ungrateful when we experience trials because we know that God sees perfectly the end result (cf. 1 Pet. 4:12–13).

Ephesians 5:18-20 reiterates the command to be thankful: "And do not get drunk with wine, for that is dissipation, but be filled with the Spirit, speaking to one another in psalms and hymns and spiritual songs, singing and making melody with your heart to the Lord; always giving thanks for all things in the name of our Lord Jesus Christ to God, even the Father." Such a well-rounded, consistent attitude of praise and thanksgiving is not possible in our own strength. But if we allow God's indwelling Spirit to work through us and empower us, He will enable us to give thanks every day for whatever the Lord brings into our lives.

Without the person and work of Christ, we could not even consider the practical expression of gratitude. But because our Lord means so much to us, Paul instructs us to be grateful in ways consistent with who Jesus is and what He has done.

Of course, the ultimate object of all our thankfulness is God the Father. We cannot ignore the crucial truth that God desires continual offerings of thanks (e.g., Ps. 30, 92, 95, 98, 100, 105, 118; Heb. 13:15). The very inclusion of God's name in Ephesians 5:20 should be a reminder of His kindness to His children and the endless number of blessings He faithfully sends them (Jas. 1:17).

In addition to the direct commands in 1 Thessalonians 5 and Ephesians 5, Paul's other letters are filled with more inferential references to the importance of gratitude in the life of the church.

Amid the context of other issues, 1 Corinthians 14:16-17 says, "If you bless in the spirit only, how will the one who fills the place of the ungifted say the 'Amen' at your giving of thanks, since he does not know what you are saying? For you are giving thanks well enough, but the other man is not edified." Apparently the church at Corinth, and other churches Paul established, had a public giving of thanks as a regular segment of their worship services.

Paul continued to remind the Corinthian believers of the importance of gratitude. Second Corinthians 4:15 says, "For all things are for your sakes, that the grace which is spreading to more and more people may cause the giving of thanks to abound to the glory of God." This really summarizes the purpose of Paul's entire ministry. He endured all the sufferings and hardships so that the Gospel would be widely proclaimed and much thanksgiving would redound to the glory of God.

As the message of saving grace spreads, it's as if each conversion adds a new member to the divine choir in which everyone is always overwhelmed with an attitude of thanks. And that should be the norm for believers. It is so disappointing to be around professing Christians who always seem to be stressed out, dissatisfied, depressed, and generally unhappy about their circumstances. Instead, they ought to be following the scriptural pattern and giving thanks daily for God's great grace.

Further on in 2 Corinthians, as Paul summarizes his teaching on giving, he also relates those principles to the subject of thanksgiving:

> *And God is able to make all grace abound to you, that always having all sufficiency in everything, you may have an abundance for*

every good deed; as it is written, "He scattered abroad, He gave to the poor, His righteousness abides for ever." Now He who supplies seed to the sower and bread for food, will supply and multiply your seed for sowing and increase the harvest of your righteousness; you will be enriched in everything for all liberality, which through us is producing thanksgiving to God. For the ministry of this service is not only fully supplying the needs of the saints, but is also overflowing through many thanksgivings to God. Because of the proof given by this ministry they will glorify God for your obedience to your confession of the gospel of Christ, and for the liberality of your contribution to them and to all, while they also, by prayer on your behalf, yearn for you because of the surpassing grace of God in you. Thanks be to God for His indescribable gift!

—9:8-15

That passage concludes Paul's section of instruction on Christian giving, and specifically on the Corinthians' role in the offering that was being collected for the poor saints in Jerusalem. In summary, Paul says that when believers generously invest in God's kingdom, God pours back rich dividends, and believers thank Him, which brings much glory to His name. Gratitude is actually multiplied, which brings even more glory to God. For example, here in 2 Corinthians 9 the church was taking believers' money, which would be translated into ministry that would cause other believers— the Jewish Christians in Jerusalem—to say thanks. The Jews were going to thank God that the Corinthians' salvation was genuine because it was being reflected in the generosity of their contribution. God is worthy to be thanked, and He desires to hear our thanks in everything.

In summary, as we read Paul's letters, it is evident that, under the guidance of the Holy Spirit, he continually underscored the command that believers must always manifest gratitude. The apostle regularly related this essential pillar of Christian character to every aspect of behavior, as the following passages clearly reveal (emphases added):

Be anxious for nothing, but in everything by prayer and supplication with thanksgiving let your requests be made known to God.

—*Phil. 4:6*

As you therefore have received Christ Jesus the Lord, so walk in Him, having been firmly rooted and now being built up in Him and established in your faith, just as you were instructed, and overflowing with gratitude.

—*Col. 2:6-7*

And let the peace of Christ rule in your hearts, to which indeed you were called in one body; and be thankful. *Let the word of Christ richly dwell within you, with all wisdom teaching and admonishing one another with psalms and hymns and spiritual songs,* singing with thankfulness *in your hearts to God. And whatever you do in word or deed, do all in the name of the Lord Jesus,* giving thanks *through Him to God the Father.*

—*Col. 3:15-17*

Masters [employers], grant to your slaves [employees] justice and fairness, knowing that you too have a Master in heaven. Devote yourselves to prayer, keeping alert in it with an attitude of thanksgiving.

—*Col. 4:1-2*

HINDRANCES TO GRATITUDE

When we find ourselves always struggling to have an attitude of thankfulness, we need to consider what might be hindering us.

First, an absence of gratitude may well mean that *we are not actually saved.* If we can find no cause in our heart for consistent thanksgiving to God, perhaps we need to be born from above (see again 2 Cor. 13:5).

A second thing that can hinder a grateful attitude is *doubt about God's sovereign power.* If we are unaware of or do not accept the truth that God controls all things, that He is all-wise and all-knowing, that He truly loves us as His own, or that He genuinely has our best interests in mind and sincerely wants to conform us to the image of His Son, then we are not likely to be thankful. Even if we do understand these truths, we can forget some of them, and that also prevents us from being grateful.

Meditating on a powerful but often overlooked passage such as 1 Chronicles 29:10-14 can do much to remedy any doubts or forgetfulness we may have concerning the Lord. God's sovereignty was part of David's great prayer of thanksgiving and commitment after the people so generously gave of their wealth for the building of the Temple:

> *So David blessed the LORD in the sight of all the assembly; and David said, "Blessed art Thou, O LORD God of Israel our father, forever and ever. Thine, O LORD, is the greatness and the power and the glory and the victory and the majesty, indeed everything that is in the heavens and the earth; Thine is the dominion, O LORD, and Thou dost exalt Thyself as head over all. Both riches and honor come from Thee, and Thou dost rule over all, and in Thy hand is power and might; and it lies in Thy hand to make great, and to strengthen everyone. Now therefore, our God, we thank Thee, and praise Thy glorious name. But who am I and who are my people that we should be able to offer as generously as this? For all things come from Thee, and from Thy hand we have given Thee."*

Selfishness and worldliness can also be major hindrances to an attitude of thankfulness. Those sins can keep us from gratitude in essentially the same way as false expectations and pride prevent us from rejoicing. Selfishness is never satisfied with what God has provided. That attitude places our will before God's and demands that God fulfill our every desire.

Selfishness is most often motivated by worldly culture, which claims that its pleasures, possessions, places, pursuits, prestige, and people are the real keys to happiness. If greed and materialism drive us, we'll have great difficulty being thankful because we'll always want more, and what we do have will never be just right. However, if we humbly submit to whatever God's will is for us and believe that He will give us what we need when we need it, it is much easier for us to thank Him at all times.

Selfishness and unrealistic expectations lead to another attitude that hinders thankfulness—*a critical spirit*. We become critical when we think we ought to control everything. But when we can't always manipulate the results we desire (cf. Jas. 4:13-16), we begin to view everything negatively and find fault with everyone else. If unchecked, such an attitude will become a horribly corrosive habit that destroys our thankfulness and eats away at every other aspect of our spirituality.

Impatience is another hindrance to gratitude. The concern here is not with what we want or don't want, but impatience with God's timing. We need to allow God to unfold His purposes according to His schedule and to be thankful for His plan (see Ps. 37:7; 40:1; Eccl. 7:8; Luke 8:15; 1 Thess. 5:14; Titus 2:2; Heb. 12:1; 2 Pet. 1:6; Rev. 2:2-3).

Being spiritually lukewarm is another way to dampen gratitude. If we lack zeal for God, diligence in His Word, passion in prayer, interest in worship, and a disciplined stewardship over the use of our time, we will quickly lose reason and motivation to give God thanks. And if that sin is not repented of, the consequences of a lukewarm attitude can be far more serious than a loss of gratitude. The Lord Jesus, in His letter to the church in Laodicea, issues this sobering warning to us: "I know your deeds, that you are neither cold nor hot; I would that you were cold or hot. So because you are lukewarm, and neither hot nor cold, I will spit you out of My mouth" (Rev. 3:15-16).

Finally, the strongest attitude that militates against thankfulness is *rebellion*. Several years ago I received a letter from a woman who wanted me to write to her husband, who had been rebelling against God for fourteen years. At one time he had supposed God wanted him to become a preacher. But after being involved in a small church, something didn't go his way, and that made him bitter toward God.

As a result, he was so angry that he had not even entered that church or any other church in fourteen years. Instead of indulging in the sin of bitterness and rebellion, he should have prayerfully come to the Lord with questions such as, "God, what are you saying to me through this trial? What are You trying to show me? What can I learn and how can I be thankful for it?" But he allowed his sin to make him a useless minister who harmed his wife and others and to stop him from thanking God (cf. Eph. 4:31; Heb. 12:15).

PAUL'S EXAMPLE OF CONTENTMENT

All those hindrances to gratitude can impair a Christian's relationship to God, ruin his fellowship with other believers, and ultimately destroy a church. That's why it's so crucial that we remain spiritually vigilant and guard against any attitude that would prevent us from being grateful to God for all He's provided in our lives.

The best way we can maintain an attitude of thankfulness is to be content, which basically means to be satisfied with who we are in Christ, what God has given us, and what circumstances He has placed us in. First of all, contentment means obeying Scripture's command regarding it: "Let your character be free from the love of money, being content with what you have; for He Himself has said, 'I will never desert you, nor will I ever forsake you'" (Heb. 13:5).

Contentment can also be learned by following the example of the apostle Paul, who instructed Timothy to have it (1 Tim. 6:6-8) and practiced it in his own life: "Not that I speak from want; for I have learned to be content in whatever circumstances I am. I know how to get along with humble means, and I also know how to live in prosperity; in any and every circumstance I have learned the secret of being filled and going hungry, both of having abundance and suffering need" (Phil. 4:11-12).

That is the perfect description of the contented man. However, Paul's contentment was not the result of perfect circumstances. As Paul wrote to the Philippians, he was imprisoned in Rome. His gospel preaching, which had stirred up so much trouble among the

Jews and Gentiles, led to his imprisonment in a private room in which he was continuously chained to a Roman soldier. The apostle was in extremely sparse conditions, with access to only the bare necessities. And being chained to a soldier was probably even worse than being in his own cell or a cell with other prisoners. Paul had no freedom, mobility, or privacy, and in his isolation from friends and coworkers he was constantly reminded of his situation. As he wrote Philippians 4:11-12, every movement of his hand clanked the chain with which he was linked to a soldier.

But in spite of the adversity of his imprisonment, Paul was able to say, "I have learned to be content." That makes him a role model of contentment.

In Philippians 4:11 Paul uses the simple Greek word for "content" that means to have enough or to be sufficient. It also refers to someone who doesn't need help of any kind. Outwardly it seems ridiculous that Paul, who had nothing, could confidently assert that he needed nothing. Yet by God's grace he had learned to be content.

Furthermore, in verse 12 Paul added, "I have learned the secret." In the Greek, this expression means to be initiated into the inner secrets of a religion. In Paul's day it referred to learning the secrets of one of the various mystery religions. In essence, Paul had learned the secret of contentment. That secret eludes most people, but not so for us as believers if we would just maintain the attitude of thankfulness.

The secret of how to be content need not elude us if we realize some of the principles the apostle Paul followed (see also Heb. 13:5). Primarily, he didn't worry about sorting out the meaning of every difficult situation because he knew that God's providence was in operation: "It is God who is at work in you, both to will and to work for His good pleasure" (Phil. 2:13). Paul was also firmly committed to what the writer of Proverbs had said centuries earlier: "The mind of man plans his way, but the LORD directs his steps" (16:9); "Many are the plans in a man's heart, but the counsel of the LORD, it will stand" (19:21).

Paul knew that the inspired narratives of the Old Testament demonstrated again and again the sovereignty of God through all circumstances. God used Joseph's slavery in Egypt to elevate him to prime minister so he could preserve Israel. God worked through Ruth to produce the line of David, which ultimately led to the birth of the Messiah. And God placed Esther in a pagan king's palace to stop a conspiracy that would have wiped out the Jewish people. And now Paul knew from his own experience that God was in control of everything, which resulted in his complete contentment and thanksgiving.

Paul's sense of contentment was also developed by other important guidelines, notably his willingness and ability to be satisfied with very little (1 Tim. 6:6-8), to live above life's circumstances (2 Cor. 12:10), to rely solely on God's power and provision (Gal. 2:20; Eph. 3:16; Phil. 4:13), and to be completely preoccupied with the well-being of others (Phil. 2:3-4; 4:17). (For a fuller discussion of contentment, see my book *Anxiety Attacked* [Wheaton, Ill.: Victor Books, 1993], 107-120.)

Those aspects of contentment help reinforce the attitude of Christian thankfulness. It was enough for the apostle Paul that God had arranged everything in his life and had given him all spiritual blessings and that He was showing Himself faithful and powerful in life's circumstances. Paul could easily agree with the psalmist's words, "My flesh and my heart may fail; but God is the strength of my heart and my portion forever" (Ps. 73:26). And he concluded his teaching to the Philippians with these statements of promise and praise: "My God shall supply all your needs according to His riches in glory in Christ Jesus. Now to our God and Father be the glory forever and ever. Amen" (4:19-20). There is equal reason for every Christian today to be content and always filled with thanksgiving and praise to God.

10

THE COURAGE
TO BE STRONG

In western society today there's a great emphasis on fitness and strength. Many people work out regularly and strive to eat a healthy diet. And those who don't are regularly reminded by advertisers that it's never too late for them to change to a healthier lifestyle. Even many people who don't exercise regularly are concerned about their health. So they do everything possible to minimize their intake of rich foods and to ensure that their food and beverage are uncontaminated. They also try to avoid exposure to infectious disease.

If strength is a prime concern regarding our physical health, it ought to be an even greater concern when it comes to our spiritual health. If the Body of Christ is to function as God wants, we need to know what constitutes Christian strength and what it looks like in action.

WHAT IS SPIRITUAL STRENGTH?

Spiritual strength for believers is essentially an attitude of courage, and it includes such virtues as courage of conviction, courage to be uncompromising, courage to confront error and false doctrine, and courage to face intimidation and persecution and still remain true to what is right.

A strong Christian is one who lives by principle rather than whim or opinion. He doesn't always seek the easy path or safe place but faces various challenges, takes serious risks when necessary, and stands firm against opposition to the truth. He is decisive and has fixed purposes and goals, and he moves forward even if it's a painful struggle at times.

Strength is a virtue greatly needed in today's church, in this era of vacillation, compromise, and weakness. We live in a time in which many within the church are unwilling to hold strong doctrinal convictions because they think they'll come across as unloving. But that's not what the prophets, apostles, and Reformers would have done because it's not scriptural. The church does not need weak pastors preaching weak messages to weak congregations—it needs strength of character derived from a biblical foundation.

First Corinthians 16:13-14 is a rather simple exhortation, but it is an excellent summary of spiritual strength: "Be on the alert, stand firm in the faith, act like men, be strong. Let all that you do be done in love."

The translation "act like men" in verse 13 is somewhat ambiguous and does not convey the original meaning as well as it could. The Greek verb more literally says, "Conduct yourself in a courageous way." However, "act like men" is how the verb is rendered, most likely because various translators knew that being courageous in ancient times was synonymous with being a man. From Old Testament times to the beginning of the industrial age, being a man meant carving out life in a difficult environment. That involved clearing out wilderness land, constructing buildings by hand, plowing fields manually, and constantly protecting your family from raids by other tribes. All of that meant men had to be physically strong every day.

That portrait of rigorous effort and daily physical exertion in nearly every aspect of life is difficult for us to identify with. In modern culture, most men are accustomed to working in professional and service-related occupations that require more mental than physical exertion. In a sense we have redefined the role of men to be quite different from what it was in Paul's day. Therefore, it is helpful to have additional illustrations of the verb "act like men." Even though there are no other New Testament uses of the word, the Greek translation of the Old Testament provides many examples.

The expression appears twice in Deuteronomy 31:6-7—"'Be strong and courageous, do not be afraid or tremble at them, for the LORD your God is the one who goes with you. He will not fail you or forsake you.' Then Moses called to Joshua and said to him in the sight of all Israel, 'Be strong and courageous, for you shall go with this people into the land which the LORD has sworn to their fathers to give them, and you shall give it to them as an inheritance.'" First Moses, as he prepared to turn over the leadership of Israel to Joshua, instructed the people to have strength and courage going into the Promised Land because God would lead them. Then he gave the same charge specifically to Joshua.

Just prior to his death, David exhorted his son Solomon in a similar manner: "I am going the way of all the earth. Be strong, therefore, and show yourself a man. And keep the charge of the LORD your God, to walk in His ways, to keep His statutes, His commandments, His ordinances, and His testimonies, according to what is written in the law of Moses, that you may succeed in all that you do and wherever you turn" (1 Kings 2:2-3). Notice that verse 3 tells how one can be strong and courageous: by being a person of the Word and obeying all that God has revealed in His law.

Other passages prove that the mandate to be strong and courageous is a very common Old Testament expression (see Deut. 31:23; 2 Sam. 10:9-13; 1 Chron. 22:11-13; 2 Chron. 32:6-8; Ps. 27:14). The text that richly captures the essence of it better than any other is Joshua 1:5-9:

> *"No man will be able to stand before you all the days of your life. Just as I have been with Moses, I will be with you; I will not fail you or forsake you. Be strong and courageous, for you shall give this people possession of the land which I swore to their fathers to give them. Only be strong and very courageous; be careful to do according to all the law which Moses My servant commanded you; do not turn from it to the right or to the left, so that you may have success wherever you go. This book of the law shall not depart from your mouth, but you shall meditate on it day and night, so that*

you may be careful to do according to all that is written in it; for then you will make your way prosperous, and then you will have success. Have I not commanded you? Be strong and courageous! Do not tremble or be dismayed, for the Lord your God is with you wherever you go."

In summary, to be strong and courageous means to live out one's convictions, which are found in God's revealed Word. The Lord has paved the way for us—He is with us (v. 5). Our cause is righteous (v. 6)—we just need to be faithful by having strength and courage (vv. 6, 7, 9).

Christians certainly need to be inspired and motivated to follow the various Old Testament examples regarding strength and courage. But something much more profound is involved in our fulfilling those mandates, as articulated by the apostle Paul's prayer for the Ephesian believers: "For this reason, I bow my knees before the Father, from whom every family in heaven and on earth derives its name, that He would grant you, according to the riches of His glory, to be strengthened with power through His Spirit in the inner man" (Eph. 3:14-16). So, while the call to be strong and courageous is a command, it can be obeyed only in the wondrous, mysterious power of the indwelling Holy Spirit. That means we must be filled and controlled by the Spirit as we seek to live consistently by the convictions that arise from our Spirit-led understanding of Scripture.

PORTRAITS OF A STRONG CHRISTIAN

God's Word has provided us with a solid definition of spiritual strength, and every mature believer knows almost intuitively what that definition entails. But the question remains, how do we apply the truths about strength? How do we take the numerous scriptural exhortations and translate them into an effective spiritual attitude that results in righteous living?

The apostle Paul helps us get a practical handle on the concept of strength in his instructions to Timothy:

You therefore, my son, be strong in the grace that is in Christ Jesus. And the things which you have heard from me in the presence of many witnesses, these entrust to faithful men, who will be able to teach others also. Suffer hardship with me, as a good soldier of Christ Jesus. No soldier in active service entangles himself in the affairs of everyday life, so that he may please the one who enlisted him as a soldier. And also if anyone competes as an athlete, he does not win the prize unless he competes according to the rules. The hard-working farmer ought to be the first to receive his share of the crops. Consider what I say, for the Lord will give you understanding in everything.

—2 Tim. 2:1-7

Timothy was Paul's protégé in the faith, a true disciple who knew the apostle's heart as well as anyone. Paul had designated Timothy to take over his ministry after he was gone. But in the meantime, following Paul's first imprisonment, he asked Timothy to meet him at Ephesus, the site of one of the strongest, most influential churches Paul had planted.

While he was in prison, Paul had learned that the church leadership in Ephesus had become corrupt, that the members were abandoning their duties, and that ungodliness had entered the fellowship. So Paul solicited Timothy's help in setting the church back on the right track (cf. 1 Tim. 1:3).

After Paul dealt with some of the weightier problems at Ephesus, such as the excommunication of the heretical pastors Hymenaeus and Alexander, he departed for ministry in Macedonia and left the younger Timothy to straighten out the various other problems. After he left, Paul did send a letter to Timothy detailing major corrections that were to be made (the letter we know as 1 Timothy).

As Timothy began to implement Paul's instructions, he encountered hostile resistance from within the church and intense persecution from the outside. Many said he was too young and inexperienced. And he struggled within himself with the temptations of youthful lusts. In addition to all that, Timothy's aggressive and argumentative style probably caused him to lose ground in his efforts, and he begin to seriously doubt his role as a godly example to the Ephesians.

As a result, Timothy got caught in the downward spiral of the church at Ephesus. He started to abandon his ministry and became spiritually weak—so much so that Paul had to remind Timothy of the validity of his faith and encourage him not to let his gifts of preaching, evangelizing, and church leadership fall into disuse (2 Tim. 1:5-7). Timothy may have become so weak that he was hesitating to identify with Christ and was wavering in his doctrine. Apparently he wanted to avoid persecution from unbelievers and felt more comfortable about backing away from battling the opponents within the church (see vv. 8, 13-14).

Therefore, Paul opens 2 Timothy 2 by calling for his younger partner in ministry to exercise strong spiritual leadership. Because the apostle would soon pass from the scene, he knew it was crucial for Timothy to step forward and be a role model for others. And to demonstrate that in practical, tangible terms, Paul presents Timothy (and us) with a series of pictures or analogies to describe the strong Christian.

The Christian as Teacher

Paul begins his descriptive sequence by urging Timothy to be a teacher: "The things which you have heard from me in the presence of many witnesses, these entrust to faithful men, who will be able to teach others also" (2:2). Teaching others improves our own understanding of Scripture, and it also strengthens and extends the base of our convictions. There are four basic reasons these benefits accrue for the faithful teacher.

First, *if we wish to teach the Word effectively, we have to study it.* Teaching thus provides real incentive to dig into Scripture with full devotion. As a rule, we don't study it with the same level of thoroughness and dedication when we don't have to teach it. And that's the point—teaching will motivate us to maintain good Bible study habits.

The teacher's need to study will also aid his overall self-discipline.

It will force him to prepare far enough ahead so he will be ready when it's time to teach. A number of years ago several students in a seminary class I taught learned a painful lesson about the value of preparation.

I gave the class an assignment at the beginning of the semester and said it would be due in about one month. When that date arrived and it was time to turn in the assignment, three or four men in the class begged me for a brief extension on the due date, citing extenuating circumstances for not having their papers ready.

When I said they could not have an extension of the deadline and would therefore have to fail the assignment, they were all naturally dismayed and disappointed. Yet each one of those men admitted that he had remembered the original deadline but simply presumed I would allow a grace period for turning in the assignment late.

I told them that if they learned nothing else from the class, I hoped they would at least learn that a pastor has to have his sermon ready each Sunday, not the following Tuesday. And some of them in more recent years have told me that experience was the best lesson they ever learned.

The second reason we benefit by teaching others is that *our preparation clarifies the truth in our own hearts and minds*. It compels us to go beyond a devotional reading of the Scripture to a level at which we can understand a passage and explain its truths to others. If we study well in preparing to teach, we will gain a precision of understanding that will allow us to clarify the truth for our students.

Third, preparing to teach is beneficial because *it forces us to reach conclusions about what's important*. As we study, we have to identify the key points in the material and decide what the main emphasis will be and how to best articulate it.

Finally, being a teacher is beneficial because *it places us in a position of accountability*. When we teach others, even if it's just one person, we publicly declare the importance of what we've said and demonstrate that we want our students to embrace the same truths. We are making them accountable for what they've heard and at the same time making ourselves accountable to them to help us practice what we teach.

If we would be strong Christians, we need to teach others,

whether it's someone in our family, a fellow believer who is less mature, or a new believer. Passing on sound doctrine and practice is an integral part of preparing the next generation of faithful Christians.

During my years as a pastor, I've greatly benefited from my regular role as a teacher. I remember what I teach from God's Word and know what I believe because it's been refined and reinforced in the crucible of consistent study. That promotes real ownership over the material I present so that teaching becomes a fabric of my life and the substance of my spiritual strength. And I'm always held accountable. Any misstatement or deviation, real or apparent, that causes people to think I'm being inconsistent with my previous teachings results in letters, phone calls, faxes, and E-mail messages to my office.

Being a teacher of God's Word in informal settings does not require that we have the gift of teaching. It simply means recognizing the responsibility we have to impart truth to others so they too can understand it. That's how we form our convictions and acquire spiritual strength.

The Christian as Soldier

The next image Paul presents to Timothy of the strong Christian is that of the soldier: "Suffer hardship with me, as a good soldier of Christ Jesus. No soldier in active service entangles himself in the affairs of everyday life, so that he may please the one who enlisted him as a soldier" (2 Tim. 2:3-4). We need to realize from the start of the Christian life that we are engaged in serious spiritual warfare and a great ideological battle. We will be dealing with people of the world who don't know Christ: "The god of this world [Satan] has blinded the minds of the unbelieving, that they might not see the light of the gospel of the glory of Christ" (2 Cor. 4:4). And the power of that world system presses down on unbelievers with an appeal to their lust, covetousness, and pride (1 John 2:16). That system has also erected formidable ideological fortresses behind which people can hide all kinds of false religions, false philosophies, and unscriptural worldviews.

Therefore, the believer's responsibility is to assault the kingdom of darkness and, with the Lord's help, rescue souls lost in that darkness and bring them into the kingdom of light. As the apostle Jude says, we are to be about the duty of "snatching them out of the fire" (Jude 23).

Paul's exhortation to Timothy about being a soldier for Christ follows the spiritual warfare paradigm and describes how believers can be effective soldiers and thus strong Christians. Because we are soldiers, we shouldn't be surprised if the effort is strenuous and the tasks challenging. Neither should we be startled and retreat when encountering conflict. Such things reflect the nature of warfare, and all genuine believers are engaged in a war.

Those difficult aspects of spiritual warfare make up the first aspect of Christian soldiering: *we must suffer hardship*. That means great risk is involved, and we have to get our priorities aligned and put our lives on the line for the cause of Jesus Christ. That will require us to exercise other traits, such as being watchful (Luke 12:35-40), understanding Satan's schemes (Eph. 6:11; 1 Pet. 5:8-9); and exercising discernment (1 Thess. 5:20-21; 1 John 4:1; cf. Acts 17:11). Everything demands the vigilance and energy of an actual soldier on reconnaissance.

A second lifestyle component of the good soldier for Christ is that *he or she does not get entangled in the everyday affairs of life*. In the secular realm, when a person is called to active military service he has to change all previous relationships and make the military a full-time job. He has no private or personal life to speak of; he dresses in a uniform, lives in a special environment, and is under the authority and control of his superiors for his entire tour of duty.

Being a soldier in the spiritual realm is very similar. We have been called to serve the supreme commander, the Lord Himself, and that's a full-time, lifelong commitment. It might take us to severe levels of suffering, as in Paul's case, or a much lighter level of hardship, as is true for most of us.

It's not that Christians don't work or go to school; but when they are on the job, in the classroom, or in the neighborhood, they are soldiers for Jesus Christ. Their primary concern is the spiritual battle, whether the issues they confront are the false ideologies that trap people in sin and error or the sins and false doctrines that bring believers under Satan's influence. Wherever believers are and whatever the issue is, they can't set aside the duty of being a Christian soldier.

Finally, the true soldier of Jesus Christ *strives to please his commander, the one who enlisted him as a soldier*. If we are engaged in spiritual warfare, it's clear there is really only one person we are answerable to, and that is God, our commander. The apostle Paul, the other apostles, the prophets, and all faithful servants of the Lord have looked forward to the day when they will face Him and hear the words, "Well done, good and faithful slave [servant, soldier]" (Matt. 25:21-23; cf. v. 34). That should also be our incentive, as well as the desire to reiterate Paul's words, "I have fought the good fight, I have finished the course, I have kept the faith; in the future there is laid up for me the crown of righteousness, which the Lord, the righteous Judge, will award to me on that day; and not only to me, but also to all who have loved His appearing" (2 Tim. 4:7-8).

The Christian as Athlete

The third picture Paul gives Timothy of the strong Christian is that of the athlete: "If any one competes as an athlete, he does not win the prize unless he competes according to the rules" (2 Tim. 2:5). The noun "athlete" in the original Greek actually comes from the verb *athleō*, which means to engage in a contest or to contend in public games. (In the *King James Version*, the word's use in this verse is translated "strive for masteries.")

The meaning of *athleō* indicates the first distinctive about an athlete, which is that *he or she competes to win*. Playing to win is one of the essentials of all sports and athletics. Anything less is at best a disappointment and at worst a shame and dishonor.

The apostle Paul was interested in helping other believers to understand what he knew—that striving for an ultimate goal is necessary for the strong Christian. He or she runs to receive the reward, as we saw in Matthew 25:21-23 and 2 Timothy 4:7-8. Paul further explains the reason and manner for striving as we run the race in the

Christian life: "Do you not know that those who run in a race all run, but only one receives the prize? Run in such a way that you may win. And everyone who competes in the games exercises self-control in all things. They then do it to receive a perishable wreath, but we an imperishable" (1 Cor. 9:24-25).

Strong Christians will work hard in the spiritual arena when they understand that spiritual and eternal goals are at stake. Earlier, in his first letter to Timothy, Paul gave this excellent instruction: "Discipline yourself for the purpose of godliness; for bodily discipline is only of little profit, but godliness is profitable for all things, since it holds promise for the present life and also for the life to come. It is a trustworthy statement deserving full acceptance. For it is for this we labor and strive, because we have fixed our hope on the living God, who is the Savior of all men, especially of believers" (4:7-10). Strong believers have their affections set on heaven, not on earth, and that heavenly goal is what makes them work hard.

The honest, hardworking athlete will have one other character virtue: *he will compete according to the rules.* He won't be like some of the athletes at recent Olympic games who have cheated and terribly dishonored not only themselves but the countries they represented.

For example, we now know that over the course of four or five Olympics during the past twenty-five years women athletes, notably swimmers, from the former East Germany used steroids and probably other performance-enhancing drugs to gain tremendous strength advantages over the competition. The 1996 Olympics in Atlanta revealed that many athletes from Mainland China had engaged in similar rules violations. And there was the famous case of the great Canadian sprinter Ben Johnson, who violated the rules at the 1988 Seoul Olympics. After a brilliant Gold-Medal performance in the 100-meter dash, he tested positive for illegal substances and was stripped of his medal.

I've always respected those professional golfers who report some minor violation they commit during a tournament. If they mark their scorecard incorrectly or improperly move a ball on the course, they can be penalized one or more strokes. That kind of penalty often leads to a lower finish in the standings and costs them tens of thousands of dollars in prize money. But they listen to their conscience and are honest about it. It would be wonderful if God's people, especially His leaders, would always display such integrity and run the race according to the rules He has laid out.

Strong Christians will heed the apostle Paul's words in 1 Corinthians 9:26-27: "Therefore I run in such a way, as not without aim; I box in such a way, as not beating the air; but I buffet my body and make it my slave, lest possibly, after I have preached to others, I myself should be disqualified." That kind of self-discipline is a necessary part of spiritual athletics. We have to bring our bodies into subjection so our flesh, with its evil desires, does not dominate us and lead us into some sin that will divert us and others from the true goal of spiritual warfare. But when we honor the Lord Jesus Christ and focus on the eternal reward that awaits all who are faithful, that will bring out only our best efforts of spiritual service.

The Christian as Farmer

The final image Paul gives to Timothy of the strong Christian is that of the hardworking farmer (2 Tim. 2:6). And the spiritual farmer's first task is to be busy *sowing the seed of God's Word*, as the sower did in the Parable of the Soils (Matt. 13:3-23).

Jesus' parable illustrates four types of soils (people) and their various levels of receptivity to the seed (God's Word). Three soils were bad and had negative responses, and one soil was good and had a positive response. Some soils are hard and immediately reject the truth. Some are stony and shallow; they receive the Word with temporary joy but let it slip away under the heat of tribulation. Still other soils are weedy, and they too receive the seed temporarily, but the deceitfulness of riches and the noxious weeds of worldly materialism soon take over and choke out the fruit of the Word.

The good soil is productive, but at three different levels—thirty-, sixty-, and a hundredfold.

The most fascinating thing about this parable is that it says nothing about the skill of the sower. It completely undercuts the contemporary notion that in order to be effective in evangelism, Christians have to use the right formula or implement a certain program that employs the appropriate "seeker-friendly" technique. Instead, the issue is the condition of the soils. That point can be underscored by an additional illustration. Imagine an experienced farmer sowing seed with great skill and dexterity. Every time he scatters seed, it falls almost perfectly into the furrows of the field. At the same time his five- or six-year-old son follows behind him and awkwardly tries to duplicate his father's skill. But his pudgy hand and short fingers errantly toss seed on his father's head and down his father's back, with other clumps landing here and there, missing the furrows. But some of the seed thrown by the son does land in good soil, and it does produce a crop.

That story illustrates the principle that whenever seed hits good soil, it produces fruit, whether the seed was thrown by a skilled or unskilled sower. The spiritual moral of Jesus' parable is that the Lord prepares the soil of people's hearts, and we distribute the seed of His Word; the more seed we distribute, the more likely it is to hit prepared soil.

Therefore, the strong Christian who is a good spiritual farmer will never pass up opportunities to spread the Gospel. He or she will work hard at it and do so whether the soil seems hard or responsive. God's Word has its own power, and believers need simply to point people to it and let it do its work. The sower has no place in tampering with or altering the seed; his role is simply to spread it.

Not only will the diligent spiritual farmer sow the seed of the Word—he will work hard at watering and building on someone else's sowing. In other words, *he will be a harvester*. As 2 Timothy 2:6 says, he "ought to be the first to receive his share of the crops." One of the primary reasons we should love to sow the seed is the exhilarating joy of the harvest. Just as the farmer rejoices when he brings in a good harvest, so the sower of God's Word praises the Lord when His Word takes root in someone's life and bears the fruit of eternal life.

Within the fourfold picture of the strong Christian, the teacher is often refreshed by his students' aspiring minds, the soldier is excited by the sights and sounds of battle, and the athlete is motivated by the challenge of competition. However, the farmer usually works alone and has no one else to stimulate him.

Most of our lives as believers are more like the farmer's than the other images of the strong Christian. There may be certain times when things are especially interesting, exciting, or rewarding, but most days involve nothing extraordinary. Whatever our daily responsibilities, however, we are promised God's blessing and reward if we are faithful. Our work and ministry may be underpaid, misunderstood, or unappreciated by coworkers—and even by fellow Christians—but that's not God's response: "Therefore, my beloved brethren, be steadfast, immovable, always abounding in the work of the Lord, knowing that your toil is not in vain in the Lord" (1 Cor. 15:58; cf. 3:13-14; Rev. 2:10).

11

SELF-DISCIPLINE: THE KEY TO VICTORY

For many people in our society, playing and watching sports is the passion of their lives. They avidly follow and root for their favorite teams, even showing up at games wearing more outlandish costumes than their children wear on Halloween. That grown men and women would attend sporting events with their faces (and sometimes bodies) painted with their team colors or wear strange-looking masks or hats reminds us that the term *fan* derives from the word *fanatic*.

The fanaticism with which many people view sports causes them to idolize prominent athletes. What makes successful athletes successful? Natural ability, good coaching, and being on a team whose personnel and playing style complement their abilities are significant factors. But there is one other, often overlooked factor that is perhaps most important of all—self-discipline. The history of sports is filled with examples of athletes whose diligent, strenuous, self-denying efforts overcame their lack of physical ability.

People in biblical times understood the relationship between sports and self-discipline because athletics were also very popular then. The Olympic Games and the Isthmian Games (held in Corinth) were eagerly anticipated. Many smaller cities held athletic meets in which local athletes took part. Therefore, the New Testament frequently uses athletic competition as a metaphor for the Christian life. Paul said to the elders of the church at Ephesus, "I do not consider my life of any account as dear to myself, in order that I may *finish my course*, and the ministry which I received from the Lord Jesus, to testify solemnly of the gospel of the grace of God" (Acts 20:24, emphasis added). In Galatians 2:2 the apostle expressed his "fear that [he] might be running, or had run, in vain." Later in that same epistle he chided the Galatians by saying: "You were running well; who hindered you from obeying the truth?" (5:7). The apostle exhorted the Philippians to be constantly "holding fast the word of life, so that in the day of Christ I may have cause to glory because I did not run in vain nor toil in vain" (Phil. 2:16). "If any one competes as an athlete," Paul reminded his young protégé Timothy, "he does not win the prize unless he competes according to the rules" (2 Tim. 2:5). Paul's own epitaph, written shortly before his martyrdom, reads: "*I have fought the good fight, I have finished the course*, I have kept the faith" (2 Tim. 4:7, emphasis added). The noble apostle triumphantly completed his race.

The writer of Hebrews also likened the Christian life to a race, exhorting his readers, "Therefore, since we have so great a cloud of witnesses surrounding us, let us also lay aside every encumbrance, and the sin which so easily entangles us, and let us run with endurance the race that is set before us" (Heb. 12:1).

But the most detailed picture of the Christian life as an athletic contest comes from Paul's first letter to the Corinthians:

> *Do you not know that those who run in a race all run, but only one receives the prize? Run in such a way that you may win. And everyone who competes in the games exercises self-control in all things. They then do it to receive a perishable wreath, but we an imperishable. Therefore I run in such a way, as not without aim; I box in such a way, as not beating the air; but I buffet my body and make it my slave, lest possibly, after I have preached to others, I myself should be disqualified.*
>
> —*9:24-27*

The only reason to run a race is to be the one who "receives the prize"; no competitor wants to finish second. That's why Paul exhorts

Christians to "run in such a way that you may win" (v. 24). How do we do that? By exercising "self-control in all things" (v. 25). In the Christian life, as in athletic competition, victory goes to the self-disciplined. World-class athletes spend a staggering amount of time in training. They may train many hours a day for several years of their lives, forcing themselves to ignore pain in order to master their sport. They do it to receive the modern equivalent of a "perishable wreath"; believers exercise self-discipline for the imperishable "crown of righteousness" (2 Tim. 4:8).

An athlete's hard training, however, will be wasted if he or she violates the rules of competition. We've all seen the frustration of Olympic skiers who accidentally missed a gate on the slalom course and were disqualified. Other athletes have deliberately cheated, bringing shame and dishonor on both themselves and their countries. "Therefore," wrote Paul in verse 26, "I run in such a way, as not without aim." He made certain he stayed on course, knowing that, as he later wrote to Timothy, "If anyone competes as an athlete, he does not win the prize unless he competes according to the rules" (2 Tim. 2:5). Paul feared lest, having "preached to others, [he himself] should be disqualified" (v. 27). He didn't want the lack of self-discipline to cause him to miss out on spiritual victory.

Self-discipline may be defined as the ability to regulate one's conduct by principle and sound judgment rather than by impulse, desire, or social custom. Rudyard Kipling's famous poem "If" captures self-discipline's essence from a purely human perspective:

> *If you can keep your head when all about you*
> *Are losing theirs and blaming it on you;*
> *If you can trust yourself when all men doubt you,*
> *But make allowance for their doubting too;*
> *If you can wait and not be tired by waiting,*
> *Or, being lied about, don't deal in lies,*
> *Or, being hated, don't give way to hating,*
> *And yet don't look too good, nor talk too wise;*

If you can dream—and not make dreams your master;
     If you can think—and not make thoughts your aim;
If you can meet with triumph and disaster
     And treat those two imposters just the same;
If you can bear to hear the truth you've spoken
     Twisted by knaves to make a trap for fools,
Or watch the things you gave your life to broken,
     And stoop and build 'em up with worn-out tools;

If you can make one heap of all your winnings
     And risk it on one turn of pitch-and-toss,
And lose, and start again at your beginnings
     And never breathe a word about your loss;
If you can force your heart and nerve and sinew
     To serve your turn long after they are gone,
And so hold on when there is nothing in you
     Except the Will which says to them: "Hold on!"

If you can talk with crowds and keep your virtue,
     Or walk with kings—nor lose the common touch;
If neither foes nor loving friends can hurt you;
     If all men count with you, but none too much;
If you can fill the unforgiving minute
     With sixty seconds' worth of distance run—
Yours is the Earth and everything that's in it,
     And—which is more—you'll be a Man, my son!

Biblically, self-discipline may be summarized in one word: obedience. To exercise self-discipline in spiritual things is to avoid evil by staying within the bounds of God's law.

Self-discipline is important in any endeavor of life. I'm grateful for my parents, coaches, professors, and others who helped me develop self-discipline in my own life. People who have the ability to concentrate, focus on their goals, and consistently stay within their priorities tend to succeed. Whether in academics, the arts, or athletics, success generally comes to the self-disciplined.

For many years I have had the privilege of knowing the renowned classical guitarist Christopher Parkening. By the time he was thirty, he had become a master of his instrument. But such mastery did not come easily or cheaply. While other children played and participated in sports, he spent several hours a day practicing the guitar. The result of that self-disciplined commitment is a proficiency on his instrument that few can match.

HOW TO DEVELOP SELF-DISCIPLINE

Since self-discipline is so important, how does one develop it? How can parents help their children develop it? Here are some practical tips that I've found helpful:

Start with small things. Clean your room at home or your desk at work. Train yourself to put things where they belong when they are out of place. Make the old adage "A place for everything and everything in its place" your motto. After you've cleaned your room or desk, extend that discipline of neatness to the rest of your house and workplace. Get yourself to the point where orderliness matters. Learn how to keep your environment clean and clear so you can function without a myriad of distractions. Such neatness will further develop self-discipline by forcing you to make decisions about what is important and what is not.

Learning self-discipline in the little things of life prepares the way for big successes. On the other hand, those who are undisciplined in small matters will likely be undisciplined in more important issues. In the words of Solomon, it is the little foxes that ruin the vineyards (Song 2:15). When it comes to a person's integrity and credibility, there are no small issues.

A famous rhyme, based on the defeat of King Richard III of England at the battle of Bosworth Field in 1485, illustrates the importance of concentrating on small details:

> *For want of a nail, a shoe was lost,*
> *For want of a shoe, a horse was lost,*

> *For want of a horse, a battle was lost,*
> *For want of a battle, a kingdom was lost,*
> *And all for want of a horseshoe nail.*

Get yourself organized. Make a schedule, however detailed or general you are comfortable with, and stick to it. Have a to-do list of tasks you need to accomplish. Using a daily planning book or a personal information manager program on your computer would be helpful. However you do it, get organized, even if all you do is jot down appointments and to-do items on a piece of scrap paper. The simple reality is that if you don't control your time, everything (and everyone) else will.

Don't constantly seek to be entertained. When you have free time, do things that are productive instead of merely entertaining. Read a good book, or listen to classical music, or take a walk, or have a conversation with someone. In other words, learn to entertain yourself with things that are challenging, stimulating, and creative. Things that are of no value except to entertain you make a very small contribution to your well-being.

Be on time. If you're supposed to be somewhere at a specific time, be there on time. "Dost thou love life?" wrote Benjamin Franklin in *Poor Richard's Almanac*, "Then do not squander time, for that is the stuff life is made of." The apostle Paul listed proper use of time as a mark of true spiritual wisdom: "Be careful how you walk, not as unwise men, but as wise, making the most of your time, because the days are evil" (Eph. 5:15-16). Being punctual marks a life that is organized. It reveals a person whose desires, activities, and responsibilities are under control, allowing him to get where he needs to be when he needs to be there. Being on time also acknowledges the importance of other people and the value of their time.

Keep your word. "Undertake not what you cannot perform," a young George Washington exhorted himself, "but be careful to keep your promise." If you say you're going to do something, do it—*when* you said you would do it and *how* you said you would do it. When you make commitments, see them through. That calls for the discipline to properly evaluate whether you have the time and capability to do something. And once you've made the commitment, self-discipline will enable you to keep it.

Do the most difficult tasks first. Most people do just the opposite, spending their time doing the easier, low-priority tasks. But when they run out of time (and energy), the difficult, high-priority tasks are left undone.

Finish what you start. Some people's lives are a sad litany of unfinished projects. In the words of poet John Greenleaf Whittier:

> *For of all sad words of tongue or pen,*
> *The saddest are these: "It might have been!"*

If you start something, finish it. Therein lies an important key to developing self-discipline.

Accept correction. Correction helps you develop self-discipline by showing you what you need to avoid. Thus, it should not be rejected but accepted gladly. Solomon wrote, "Listen to counsel and accept discipline, that you may be wise the rest of your days" (Prov. 19:20); and "He whose ear listens to the life-giving reproof will dwell among the wise. He who neglects discipline despises himself, but he who listens to reproof acquires understanding" (Prov. 15:31-32).

Practice self-denial. Learn to say no to your feelings and impulses. Occasionally deny yourself pleasures that are perfectly legitimate for you to enjoy. Skip dessert after a meal. Drink a glass of iced tea instead of having that banana split you love. Don't eat that doughnut that caught your eye. Refraining from those things will remind your body who is in charge.

Welcome responsibility. Volunteer to do things that need to be done. That will force you to have your life organized enough to have time for such projects.

These practical suggestions may not seem to involve any deep spiritual principles. Yet we cannot split our lives into the secular and the spiritual. Instead we must live every aspect of our lives to the glory of God (1 Cor. 10:31). And self-discipline cultivated in the seemingly mundane things of life will spill over into the spiritual realm.

THE MOTIVATION FOR DEVELOPING SELF-DISCIPLINE

Self-discipline is essential for spiritual victory and growth; that alone should motivate Christians to pursue it diligently. In 1 Peter 1:13 Peter wrote, "Therefore, gird your minds for action, keep sober in spirit." Peter's picture is that of a Roman soldier preparing for battle. To avoid being encumbered by his tunic, a soldier would tuck its loose ends into his sash. Spiritual victory begins with a commitment to pull together all the loose ends in our thinking.

Believers do that by keeping "sober in spirit." "Sober" in this context does not refer to not being drunk; rather, it speaks of being clear-minded and understanding priorities. To prioritize our thinking means to think about those things we ought to think about—those things that are true, honorable, right, pure, lovely, of good repute, excellent, and worthy of praise (Phil. 4:8).

A disciplined mind avoids the intoxicating allurements of the world. It is clear, with fixed and balanced priorities, resulting in moral decisiveness. People who possess a disciplined mind do not whimsically career through life in reckless self-indulgence. They live by principle, not emotion. That's why sound doctrine is so important; believers need divine truth firmly fixed in their minds, so that it controls their priorities.

In Romans 13:13-14 the apostle Paul contrasted an undisciplined mind with one controlled by biblical truth: "Let us behave properly as in the day, not in carousing and drunkenness, not in sexual promiscuity and sensuality, not in strife and jealousy. But put on the Lord Jesus Christ, and make no provision for the flesh in regard to its lusts." The opposite of careening recklessly through life, giving in to every sinful lust, impulse, and desire, is to "put on the Lord Jesus Christ." Those who have done so possess "the mind of Christ" (1 Cor. 2:16) and will think like He thinks.

To the Thessalonians Paul wrote, "Let us not sleep as others do, but let us be alert and sober . . . since we are of the day, let us be sober" (1 Thess. 5:6, 8). In his first epistle, Peter exhorted believers to be sober in their thinking for a second time: "Be of sober spirit, be on the alert. Your adversary, the devil, prowls about like a roaring lion, seeking someone to devour" (1 Pet. 5:8). A sober mind is an excellent defense against Satan's attacks.

THE BIBLICAL PRIORITIES OF A SELF-DISCIPLINED PERSON

We've already noted that self-discipline is important from a purely human perspective, and we've listed some practical principles for attaining it. But there are also biblical principles that help Christians pursue self-discipline. They all involve two things: correct thinking about a biblical truth and a commitment to obey that truth. Let's examine these foundational priorities of a self-disciplined person.

Remember Who Owns You

Our narcissistic, self-absorbed, self-centered society constantly tells us that we are the kings of our own little worlds, that we have the right to be what we want to be, to set our own goals, pursue our own dreams, choose our own lifestyles, and ignore those who tell us what to do or stand in our way. The two hallmarks of our culture are personal rights and personal freedom. But the Bible in no uncertain terms teaches the very opposite. Scripture reveals God as the rightful owner of all men because He created them and of all of us who are believers because He is our Father who purchased us.

Christians rightly take comfort in the oft-repeated biblical truth that God is their Father (see Matt. 5:16; 18:14; 23:9; Mark 11:25; 1 Thess. 1:3; 3:13; etc.). But the often overlooked corollary to that truth is that we owe God our obedience. First Peter 1:14 exhorts believers to be "obedient children." To fail to obey God is to rob Him of something that is rightfully His. "If I am a father," God demanded of rebellious, disobedient Israel, "where is My honor?" (Mal. 1:6).

Believers also belong to God because He bought them at an immeasurable cost—the death of His beloved Son, Jesus Christ. "Do you not know," Paul demanded of the Corinthians, "that your body is a temple of the Holy Spirit who is in you, whom you have from God, and that you are not your own?" (1 Cor. 6:19; cf. 7:23). In verse

20 the apostle added, "For you have been bought with a price: therefore glorify God in your body."

Peter described the price God paid to redeem believers in 1 Peter 1:18-19: "You were not redeemed with perishable things like silver or gold from your futile way of life inherited from your forefathers, but with precious blood, as of a lamb unblemished and spotless, the blood of Christ." In Acts 20:28 Paul described the church as having been "purchased with His own blood," while he wrote to the Galatians that "Christ redeemed us from the curse of the Law, having become a curse for us—for it is written, 'Cursed is everyone who hangs on a tree'" (3:13). The fearful price God paid to redeem believers was the sacrificial death of Christ on the cross, where He became a curse for us. The sinless Son of God took believers' sins upon Himself (2 Cor. 5:21), fully satisfying the demands of God's justice (Rom. 3:26) and appeasing His holy wrath against sin (Rom. 3:25).

Understanding that they don't own themselves, but that God is their rightful owner and master will motivate believers to become self-disciplined people. Christians will pursue holiness when they understand the price that Jesus Christ paid to redeem them.

That realization was at the heart of the apostle Paul's unswerving loyalty, dedication, and commitment to God. He never got over the wonder that God would choose to save him—a man who had savagely, relentlessly persecuted God's people. Even late in his life, many years after God saved him on the Damascus road, he exclaimed, "It is a trustworthy statement, deserving full acceptance, that Christ Jesus came into the world to save sinners, among whom I am foremost of all. . . . Now to the King eternal, immortal, invisible, the only God, be honor and glory forever and ever. Amen" (1 Tim. 1:15, 17).

Paul's recognition of all the implications of his salvation drove him to sacrifice his comfort, his health, and eventually his life for the God who had redeemed him. Unlike many Christians, the noble apostle never forgot that at the moment of his salvation he became God's obedient son and bond-slave. And he faithfully rendered through all the difficulties of his life the obedience due to his Father and Master. Those who, like Paul, recognize that they are not the sovereign rulers of their lives take an important step toward self-discipline.

Remember the Covenant of Salvation

It is a foundational truth, clearly and unequivocally taught throughout Scripture, that salvation is wholly a work of God. Unregenerate sinners, being dead in sin (Eph. 2:1), are helpless to save themselves (Rom. 5:6). Had God not chosen believers for salvation before the foundation of the world (Eph. 1:4; 2 Thess. 2:13), sent Christ to die for their sins (Rom. 5:8-9), and regenerated them through the power of the Holy Spirit (Titus 3:5), none would be saved.

But there is another aspect to salvation. Divine sovereignty does not eliminate human responsibility. In salvation, God promises to forgive repentant sinners, to pour out His grace on them and bring them to glory. But believers also make a promise at salvation, a promise to obey Jesus Christ as their Lord. That promise is an inescapable corollary to confessing and turning from sin. All men are either in rebellion against God or in submission to Him; there is no middle ground, no third option. Saving faith recognizes sin and therefore includes repentance; saving faith recognizes the lordship of Christ and therefore includes submission.

It is true that most people do not understand at the point of salvation all that submission to Christ's lordship entails. They do not yet have a grasp of Scripture or a complete understanding of the Christian life and all its challenges. But they do know that at salvation they committed themselves to follow Jesus Christ.

In his first epistle, Peter taught that the result of the Father's sovereign election of believers, and of the Holy Spirit's regeneration of them, is that they will "obey Jesus Christ" (1 Pet. 1:2; cf. v. 22). Unlike some today, the Bible never separates obedience from salvation. In fact, obedience is used as a synonym for salvation in such passages as Acts 6:7, Romans 1:5, 15:18, 16:26, and Hebrews 5:9.

Salvation is not merely an initial act of obedience; it also results in a *life* of obedience. In Ephesians 2:10 Paul described believers as "[God's] workmanship, created in Christ Jesus for good works, which God prepared beforehand, that we should walk in them." So inseparably linked are works to genuine saving faith that James could say, "Just as the body without the spirit is dead, so also faith without works is dead" (Jas. 2:26). Good works do not, of course, save us. But they are an inevitable consequence of our salvation.

Going back to 1 Peter 1:2, Peter then described believers as having been "sprinkled with [Christ's] blood." This picture is borrowed from the affirmation of the Mosaic covenant in Exodus 24. After hearing the covenant read, the Israelites promised to obey it (v. 7). Moses then sprinkled them with the blood of the sacrifice to seal their part of the covenant (v. 8). When Peter spoke of Christ's blood being sprinkled on believers (symbolically, not literally), he depicted their part in the covenant of salvation—obedience to God.

A self-disciplined Christian is one who remembers the pledge he made at salvation to obey God. Such a believer then has the integrity to remain true to that commitment. (See again Chapter 2.)

Recognize That Sin Violates Your Relationship to God

Sin is much more than the violation of a code. The Bible teaches that all sin is ultimately against God and violates our relationship with our heavenly Father. After his heinous sins of adultery with Bathsheba and the resultant murder of her husband, David cried out to God, "Against Thee, Thee only, I have sinned, and done what is evil in Thy sight" (Ps. 51:4). Peter exhorted believers, "If you address as Father the One who impartially judges according to each man's work, conduct yourselves in fear during the time of your stay upon earth" (1 Pet. 1:17). In other words, if you are God's child, act like it. Don't violate your intimate relationship with Him by sinning (cf. 1 Cor. 6:15-17).

Paul illustrated this principle in his epistle to the Philippians. In chapter 2 he gave the believers a series of commands (vv. 2-4, 12-18). But the apostle prefaced those commands by giving his readers the motive for obeying them—the encouragement, consolation, fellowship, affection, and compassion they enjoyed because of their relationship with God (v. 1).

Believers are to obey the commands of Scripture because breaking them violates their relationship with God. Seeing sin in that light is an important motivation for developing the self-discipline to avoid it.

Control Your Imagination

The imagination is truly a wonderful thing. It is the creative part of man, where artists conceive their art, musicians their music, and authors their books. It's where skyscrapers, bridges, and houses first take shape, before their designs show up on paper. The imagination is where people cultivate the dreams that ultimately come to fruition in their lives.

But like God's other gifts to man, the imagination can be put to perverted, sinful uses as well. For it is in the imagination that temptation is entertained, evil fantasies arise, and sinful passions are inflamed. To become a self-disciplined person, you must learn to control your imagination; it is there that the battle against sin must be fought.

James 1:14-15 exposes the origin of sin, showing how it progresses from temptation to sinful deed: "Each one is tempted when he is carried away and enticed by his own lust. Then when lust has conceived, it gives birth to sin; and when sin is accomplished, it brings forth death." Man's problem does not lie in the environment, although living in a sinful, fallen world makes exposure to temptation unavoidable. The problem is within us, in our imaginations. There the sinful circumstances, situations, thoughts, words, and concepts we are exposed to are internalized. The imagination then becomes the place where temptation is entertained and fantasies developed that, if unchecked, will produce sinful acts. The imagination plays out sinful deeds before they are ever committed (see Matt. 5:21-22, 27-28).

The imagination is where the battle against sin is won or lost. Two conflicting thoughts fight for control of the imagination when we are tempted. One thought is that sin will bring pleasure (Heb. 11:25); the other is that sin will dishonor God. Therein lies the battle. Which thought will capture the imagination, fire the emotions, and move the will?

How can we fight back against the sin that seeks to capture our imagination? The psalmist knew the answer: "Thy word I have trea-sured in my heart, that I may not sin against Thee" (Ps. 119:11). Reading the Word, studying the Word, and, above all, meditating on the Word (Josh. 1:8; Ps. 19:14; Phil. 4:8) fills our imaginations with divine truth, making it difficult for sinful temptations to get a foothold.

The spiritual battle lines are drawn. We can fill our minds with sound biblical truth and know victory over sin. Or we can allow the sinful temptations, to which we are constantly exposed, to rule unchallenged in our imaginations. That will lead to defeat in the spir-itual battle and to the tragic consequences of sin. The acronym from computer science, GIGO ("Garbage In, Garbage Out"), is also appli-cable in the spiritual life. A self-disciplined person will heed the wise counsel of Solomon: "Watch over your heart with all diligence, for from it flow the springs of life" (Prov. 4:23).

Focus on God's Causes
A final way to become self-disciplined is to shift your focus off your-self and onto God's causes. Even unbelievers will make immense, almost unbelievable sacrifices for the causes they are committed to. Can we who serve the living God do less? It is axiomatic that people whose lives matter to God are not selfish about those same lives. Jim Elliot, missionary and martyr, wrote, "He is no fool who gives what he cannot keep to gain what he cannot lose" (Elisabeth Elliot, *Shadow of the Almighty* [San Francisco: Harper & Row, 1958], 108). As Christians, we face a daunting task as God's ambassadors: bringing the life-giving message of reconciliation to a lost world (2 Cor. 5:19-20). The enormity of that challenge, if we take it seriously, will force us to discipline ourselves, for only then can we effectively serve our Master's cause. You will begin to pull together the loose ends of your life when you are no longer living for yourself.

Many today seem to think that the goal of the Christian life is for Jesus to make us healthy, wealthy, and happy. But if that's true, some-body forgot to tell the apostle Paul. Almost from the moment of his conversion on the road to Damascus, he suffered hardship, persecu-tion, and pain for the cause of Christ. The prophetic words of Jesus about him, "I will show him how much he must suffer for My name's sake" (Acts 9:16), set the course for the rest of Paul's life.

Yet, despite the suffering he endured, Paul's commitment and dedication to fulfilling the ministry to which the Lord had called him never wavered. Acts 20 finds the apostle in Miletus, a city in Asia Minor about thirty miles south of Ephesus. Hurrying to reach Jerusalem by the Day of Pentecost (v. 16), Paul bypassed Ephesus, where he had long ministered. But he could not pass up the opportunity to give one last word of encouragement and exhortation to the elders of the Ephesian church (v. 17ff.). In the context of that farewell message, Paul addressed their fears for his safety once he reached Jerusalem:

> *"And now, behold, bound in spirit, I am on my way to Jerusalem, not knowing what will happen to me there, except that the Holy Spirit solemnly testifies to me in every city, saying that bonds and afflictions await me. But I do not consider my life of any account as dear to myself, in order that I may finish my course, and the ministry which I received from the Lord Jesus, to testify solemnly of the gospel of the grace of God."*
>
> *—vv. 22-24*

There was something far beyond Paul that drove him—something so important to him that, compared to it, his life was of no value to him: to serve the cause of Christ to his dying breath. Paul's dedication to that cause produced in him tremendous self-discipline. And that self-discipline kept him on course until the end of his life (2 Tim. 4:7).

When you remember who owns you, acknowledge the covenant of obedience you made at salvation, recognize sin as a violation of your relationship with God, learn to control your imagination, and live to advance God's kingdom, you will become a self-disciplined person who pleases the Lord.

12

WORSHIPING GOD
IN SPIRIT AND IN TRUTH

Years ago an explorer attempted a difficult trek through the nearly impenetrable jungle of the upper Amazon region. Seeking to make good time, he drove his baggage carriers relentlessly forward, pushing on at a fast pace for two days. But on the third day, having reached the limits of their endurance, the men sat down beside their burdens and refused to move. Angrily, the explorer ordered them to their feet to resume the journey, but they refused to budge. Finally, in frustration he demanded an explanation from their chief. "They're waiting for their souls to catch up to their bodies," was his reply.

That story aptly illustrates the situation many Christians find themselves in. Weary from their frenetic religious activity, they need to pause and let their souls catch up with their bodies. Like Martha (cf. Luke 10:40), they are distracted with their spiritual service; like Mary, they need to sit at the Lord's feet in reverent worship (vv. 39, 42).

But worship is not a major emphasis in today's self-centered, pragmatic church. Seeking to appeal to non-Christians' felt needs, many churches have radically transformed their Sunday services. Almost anything goes: contemporary secular music, skits, elaborately staged multimedia shows, comedy acts, dancing, magic shows—anything, it would seem, except sound biblical preaching and worshiping God from the heart.

Turning the worship service into an evangelical dog-and-pony circus will inevitably result in the downplaying of worship. Worship doesn't fit into a service aimed at entertaining non-Christian "seekers" and making them feel comfortable and nonthreatened. Since it focuses on God, worship does not flourish in a man-centered atmosphere.

Making unbelievers the central focus when the church gathers together is a tragic reversal of the biblical pattern. The church is to come together primarily for worship, not evangelism; it is to collectively praise and worship God, not to entertain non-Christians. The church's goal is not to make unbelievers comfortable; in fact, it is just the opposite. When an unbeliever enters a church that worships God, "the secrets of his heart are disclosed; and so he will fall on his face and worship God, declaring that God is certainly among [its people]" (1 Cor. 14:25). Thus, worship is not an option, to be slipped into the church's life as inoffensively and unobtrusively as possible or ignored altogether; it is the very heart and soul of all that we are as Christians. In fact, my favorite definition of a Christian comes from Philippians 3:3, where the apostle Paul describes Christians as those who "worship in the Spirit of God and glory in Christ Jesus."

But a church can worship collectively only if it is made up of worshiping people, only if it is a church of Marys, not Marthas only. Note, however, that being a worshiper does not preclude serving God. The same Mary who sat reverently at Jesus' feet also performed one of the most humble acts of service recorded in Scripture (John 12:3). Service is important, but it must flow out of a worshiping heart.

THE DEFINITION OF WORSHIP

John 4:20-24 provides a good launching point for a biblical discussion of worship:

> *"Our fathers worshiped in this mountain, and you people say that in Jerusalem is the place where men ought to worship." Jesus said to her, "Woman, believe Me, an hour is coming when neither in this mountain, nor in Jerusalem, shall you worship the*

*Father. You worship that which you do not know; we worship
that which we know; for salvation is from the Jews. But an hour
is coming, and now is, when the true worshipers shall worship
the Father in spirit and truth; for such people the Father seeks to
be His worshipers. God is spirit, and those who worship Him
must worship in spirit and truth."*

This passage records a portion of the conversation between Jesus
and a Samaritan woman. Returning to Galilee after ministering in
Judea, Jesus stopped at a well near the small village of Sychar in
Samaria. Thirsty after His journey, Jesus asked the woman to draw
water so He could drink. Startled, she asked Him why He, a Jew,
would ask a despised Samaritan for a drink. Jesus then turned the conversation away from physical water to water as symbolic of eternal life.
She eagerly asked Jesus for that water, but His enigmatic response was
that she should first go and bring her husband back with her. That
simple request unmasked her sin, since having been married five
times she was now living with a man to whom she was not married.

Embarrassed at His request, she changed the subject, turning to
the hotly debated issue of where God was to be worshiped. The Jews
naturally held that God could be properly worshiped only at the temple in Jerusalem. The Samaritans opted for Mount Gerizim, not far
from Sychar, where their temple had stood before its destruction
about a century earlier. Though that temple was never rebuilt, the
Samaritans continued to worship on Mount Gerizim. The theme of
the conversation, then, was worship; the woman correctly viewed
getting her life right as an act of worship.

Worship may be defined as honor given to a superior being. Our
English word *worship* derives from the Old English word *weoroscipe*,
a compound word made up of the words for "worth" and "ship." It
thus has the connotation of ascribing worth to someone or something. The Greek word translated "worship" in John 4 is *proskunē*,
which literally means "to kiss toward," and thus "to bow down
before" or "to prostrate oneself before" a superior being.

Worship must be distinguished from ministry. Ministry comes to us from the Father, through the Son, in the power of the Holy Spirit, then flows out from us. Worship goes from us through the Spirit's power in the name of the Son back to the Father. Ministry descends to us from the Father; praise ascends from us to the Father. Ministry may be likened to the prophets who spoke to the people for God; worship can be likened to the priests who spoke to God for the people.

But ministry must not be thought of as unrelated to worship. In fact, the purpose of ministry is to enhance worship. Hearing the Word taught increases our capacity to worship God, and hearing others minister in song lifts our hearts to God in praise. We miss the point if we go to church seeking only to receive. We gather with other believers to minister to them, and even what we receive enables us to give. The Bible teaches that actions, as well as attitudes and words, may constitute worship (see Rom. 15:16; Phil. 1:11; 4:18; 1 Tim. 2:3; Heb. 13:15-16).

Worship is giving God the honor He is due. It rises from a heart filled with gratitude for God's saving power and unending goodness. "My heart overflows with a good theme," wrote the psalmist in Psalm 45:1. The Hebrew word translated "overflows" means to bubble up like boiling water spilling over the edge of a pot. The book of Psalms is divided into five books, each of which ends with a doxology. All of the truths in the psalms about God's nature and works would eventually result in an outburst of praise from worshiping hearts.

Similarly, after spending eleven chapters in Romans expounding the doctrine of salvation, Paul bursts out in praise to God:

> *Oh, the depth of the riches both of the wisdom and knowledge of God! How unsearchable are His judgments and unfathomable His ways! For who has known the mind of the Lord, or who became His counselor? Or who has first given to Him that it might be paid back to him again? For from Him and through Him and to Him are all things. To Him be the glory forever. Amen.*
>
> —11:33-36

He concluded the book of Romans with another doxology:

Now to Him who is able to establish you according to my gospel and the preaching of Jesus Christ, according to the revelation of the mystery which has been kept secret for long ages past, but now is manifested, and by the Scriptures of the prophets, according to the commandment of the eternal God, has been made known to all the nations, leading to obedience of faith; to the only wise God, through Jesus Christ, be the glory forever. Amen.

—16:25-27

Galatians 1:3-5, 1 Timothy 1:13-17, and 2 Timothy 4:18 record other instances in which Paul's heart bubbled over with praise and worship to God.

In His conversation with the Samaritan woman, Jesus set forth three foundational truths about worship: its source, its object, and its nature. Understanding those key principles will enable you to worship God as He deserves.

THE SOURCE OF WORSHIP

Where does worship originate? Jesus answered that question when He told the Samaritan woman, "An hour is coming, and now is, when the true worshipers shall worship the Father in spirit and truth; for such people the Father seeks to be His worshipers" (John 4:23). People become true worshipers of God only because He first seeks them. Jesus said in Luke 19:10, "The Son of Man has come to seek and to save that which was lost." Fallen man, being dead in sin (Eph. 2:1), is incapable of seeking God on his own. And, as Paul noted in Romans 3:10-12, no one does: "There is none righteous, not even one; there is none who understands, there is none who seeks for God; all have turned aside, together they have become useless; there is none who does good, there is not even one." For that reason Jesus declared in John 6:44, "No one can come to Me, unless the Father who sent Me draws him." Man is lost, and God is the seeker; therefore, the source of true worship is God Himself. Christians become worshipers of God at the moment of salvation, continue to worship Him throughout their lives, and (along with the holy angels) will spend eternity worshiping Him.

Worship in the Old Testament

The goal of God's redemptive plan in the Old Testament was to draw worshipers to Himself. Five simple truths, cycled repeatedly throughout the Old Testament, summarize its contents.

The Old Testament reveals God's character. It presents the greatness, majesty, wonder, and holiness of His person and works.

The Old Testament pronounces blessings on those who worship and obey God. The psalmist wrote, "Praise the LORD! How blessed is the man who fears the LORD, who greatly delights in His commandments" (Ps. 112:1).

The Old Testament pronounces curses on those who disobey and fail to worship God. Deuteronomy 28:15-20 lists some of the curses promised to Israel for her disobedience.

The Old Testament teaches the need for an ultimate sacrifice for sins. The One who would defeat Satan, sin, and death was promised as early as Genesis 3:15. And the countless lambs sacrificed under the Mosaic law pictured the ultimate sacrifice of the Lamb of God (cf. John 1:29). After His death, Jesus reiterated to His disciples the Old Testament teaching concerning Himself (Luke 24:27, 44-47).

The Old Testament teaches that the Messiah will one day establish His glorious kingdom on earth. Isaiah 11, among many other passages, depicts that coming kingdom.

All of those foundational truths should elicit worship. God's nature and works prompt us to praise Him. Those who worship the true God are blessed, while those who do not are cursed. The sacrifice of Jesus Christ, the promised Messiah, is the means God uses to redeem sinners who then become true worshipers. And the glorious kingdom, with the eternal state that follows it, will be a time of unending praise and worship of the King.

Worship is introduced in Genesis. The patriarchs—Abraham,

Isaac, and Jacob—were worshipers of God. In the Pentateuch, God commanded and regulated worship. The detailed description of the Tabernacle—encompassing almost 250 verses in Leviticus—emphasized the priority God placed on worship. The divinely ordained layout of Israel's camp during the wilderness also stressed the importance of worship. The Tabernacle was the central focus of the camp, with the various tribes camped around it on all four sides (Num. 2:2ff.). The purpose of the Mosaic law, including all the prescribed ceremonies, rituals, and sacrifices, was to regulate the worship of God. The book of Psalms was Israel's hymnbook, expressing praise and worship to God. And the mission of the prophets was to rebuke Israel's false worship and call the people back to a proper worship of the true God (see Isa. 1:11-20; Hos. 6:4-6; Amos 5:21-24; Mal. 1:6-14).

Negatively, the importance of worship in the Old Testament may be seen in the severe consequences of improper worship. Adam and Eve's failure to properly worship God led the human race into sin. Cain's inappropriate worship was rejected, after which he murdered his brother Abel in a fit of jealous rage. Misappropriating the incense used in the worship of God was punishable by death (Exod. 30:34-38). Nadab and Abihu were executed for failing to carry out their priestly duties regarding worship in the prescribed manner (Lev. 10:1-3). Saul's intrusion into the priestly functions cost him his kingship (1 Sam. 13:8-14). Uzzah failed to treat the Ark of the Covenant with the respect it was due and was killed by God for his irreverent act of worship (2 Sam. 6:6-7).

In Matthew 22, Jesus was asked to name the greatest commandment in the law. His reply summed up the purpose not only of the law, but of the entire Old Testament: "'You shall love the Lord your God with all your heart, and with all your soul, and with all your mind.' This is the great and foremost commandment. And a second is like it, 'You shall love your neighbor as yourself.' On these two commandments depend the whole Law and the Prophets" (vv. 37-40). The Law and the Prophets (a Jewish designation for the Old Testament) thus had as their ultimate purpose the elicitation of true worship.

Worship in the New Testament

The New Testament records the fulfillment of the redemptive plan foreshadowed in the Old Testament. It too emphasizes worship as the ultimate goal of salvation.

When Jesus came into the world, He came to be worshiped. Jesus received worship even before He was born, from both of John the Baptist's parents (Luke 1:41-42, 67-69). At and shortly after His birth Jesus was worshiped by angels (Heb. 1:6), shepherds (Luke 2:8-20), and the Magi (Matt. 2:1-2, 11). Even wicked King Herod displayed a false desire to worship Him (Matt. 2:8). During His ministry Jesus received worship from a leper (Matt. 8:2), a synagogue official (Matt. 9:18), His disciples (Matt. 14:33), James, John, and their mother (Matt. 20:20), a blind man whom He had healed (John 9:38), and even a demon-infested man, whose demonic tormentors knew full well who Jesus was (Mark 5:6). After His resurrection the women (Matt. 28:9) and His disciples (Matt. 28:17) offered Jesus reverential worship.

The book of Revelation closes the New Testament by giving several glimpses of the constant worship that takes place in heaven (4:10; 5:14; 7:11; 11:16; 19:4). Thus from beginning to end, the New Testament reveals God's unfolding redemptive plan to draw to Himself true worshipers (see Rom. 12:1; Phil. 3:3; Heb. 12:28).

THE OBJECT OF WORSHIP

In His conversation with the Samaritan woman, Jesus revealed two realities about God that are essential to true worship. God is to be worshiped as Father (John 4:21, 23) and as Spirit (John 4:24).

Worshiping God as Spirit

To say that God is spirit is to define His essential nature. He is not to be conceived of or represented in material terms, "for a spirit does not have flesh and bones" (Luke 24:39). Therefore, any form of idolatry is wrong and blasphemous, as is any pantheistic view that identifies God with the universe.

As a spirit, God is invisible (Col. 1:15; 1 Tim. 1:17). He cannot be seen, though He has revealed Himself through physical manifestations. In Old Testament times God revealed His presence through fire, cloud, and the *Shekinah* (the visible manifestation of God's glory; see 2 Chron. 7:1-2). The New Testament presents the ultimate revelation of God, when He became a man in the person of Jesus Christ. But God cannot be seen in His essential nature. "No man has seen God at any time," wrote the apostle John; "the only begotten God, who is in the bosom of the Father, He has explained Him" (John 1:18).

As a spirit, God is also "eternal, immortal" (1 Tim. 1:17). To say that God is eternal means He is uncreated and has always existed; to say that He is immortal means He is not subject to death and will always exist.

The Bible repeatedly points out the sinful folly of reducing God to an image or restricting Him to a specific location. To the pagan philosophers of Athens, Paul said, "We ought not to think that the Divine Nature is like gold or silver or stone, an image formed by the art and thought of man" (Acts 17:29). In 1 Kings 20:28 God rebuked the Syrians for foolishly imagining that Israel's God was restricted to the mountains. God rebuked the wicked in Psalm 50:21 for imagining that He was like they were. In Isaiah 46:5 He demanded, "To whom would you liken Me, and make Me equal and compare Me, that we should be alike?" The obvious answer is, "No one." Even the Tabernacle and the Temple contained no replications of God; though His presence was visibly manifested in those places, they contained no idols representing Him.

To properly worship God, we must worship Him as a spirit, giving praise and honor to Him for His "invisible attributes" (Rom. 1:20), such as His omnipotence, omniscience, omnipresence, immutability, eternity, love, justice, kindness, goodness, mercy, grace, righteousness, wrath, and holiness. To worship God is to extol Him for His mighty acts of creation and redemption and to gratefully acknowledge His providential care for us.

Worshiping God as Father

The Jews of Jesus' day thought of God as Father in the sense of Creator, the One who brought Israel into existence as a nation. To them, *father* was not a term of intimacy but of creation. But that is not the sense in which Jesus used the term here. When Jesus referred to God as Father, He was not referring to Him as the Father of humanity or of the nation of Israel, but as His own Father. Jesus was claiming, therefore, to bear the same essential nature as God—a claim that shocked and outraged His Jewish opponents. In the very next chapter of John's Gospel, Jesus confronted some of those opponents with this vital truth. He declared to them, "My Father is working until now, and I Myself am working" (John 5:17). Unlike many modern heretics who deny Christ's deity, Jesus' opponents understood perfectly the staggering implications of that statement. John notes, "For this cause therefore the Jews were seeking all the more to kill Him, because He . . . was calling God His own Father, making Himself equal with God" (v. 18). They viewed Jesus' claim to equality with God as blasphemy.

But Jesus defended His claim, declaring that He did the same works as the Father (v. 19), including raising the dead (v. 21) and executing judgment (v. 22). Further, Jesus' will is in perfect harmony with the Father's (v. 20), and He has life in Himself, just like the Father (v. 26). Because His words are the Father's words, His works the Father's works, His judgment the Father's judgment, His will the Father's will, and His life the Father's life, Jesus is worthy of the same honor as the Father (v. 23).

John recorded another occasion when Jesus claimed to be of the same essence as the Father. In John 10:30 Jesus said to His Jewish adversaries, "I and the Father are one." He did not merely mean He was one in purpose with the Father; if that were all He meant, He would have been claiming no more than the prophets had claimed. And once again His opponents clearly understood the implications of Jesus' claim, as their violent reaction makes clear: "The Jews took up stones again to stone Him. Jesus answered them, 'I showed you many good works from the Father; for which of them are you stoning Me?'

The Jews answered Him, 'For a good work we do not stone You, but for blasphemy; and because You, being a man, make Yourself out to be God'" (vv. 31-33).

True worship must view God as being one in essence with Jesus Christ. Or, to put it another way, true worshipers must worship Jesus as God. There is no genuine worship of God apart from the full recognition of the deity of Jesus Christ (cf. John 5:23). Those who attempt to separate the Son's deity from worship are blasphemers and place themselves under God's curse (1 Cor. 16:22).

THE NATURE OF WORSHIP

True worship not only views God as its source and object—it also avoids two deadly extremes: enthusiastic heresy and barren, lifeless orthodoxy. The Samaritans and Jews typified those extremes.

The Samaritans' worship was vital, lively, passionate, almost electric in its intensity. The destruction of their temple on Mount Gerizim a century earlier had not fazed them, and they continued to worship on that mountain in Jesus' day. In fact, a handful of devoted Samaritans are still worshiping there today.

But despite their zeal, the Samaritans' worship was marked by ignorance. Jesus told the Samaritan woman, "You [Samaritans] worship that which you do not know" (John 4:22). The Samaritans accepted only the Pentateuch (the five books of Moses—Genesis through Deuteronomy) and rejected the rest of the Old Testament. Certainly the Pentateuch contains many important truths. For example, such passages as Genesis 3:15 and Deuteronomy 18:15 led the Samaritans to anticipate the coming of the Messiah. After her conversation with Jesus, the woman returned to her village and excitedly exclaimed, "Come, see a man who told me all the things that I have done; this is not the Christ, is it?" (John 4:29). But having only the Pentateuch, there was much they could not know. Hence, Jesus characterized their worship as ignorant.

On the other hand, the Jews of Jesus' day (with the exception of the Sadducees) accepted the entire Old Testament as divinely inspired.

Jesus told the Samaritan woman, "We [Jews] worship that which we know; for salvation is from the Jews" (John 4:22). Although based on all God had revealed, the Jews' worship lacked the inner devotion to God that produced passionate worship. They tended to be coldly legalistic externalists, even hypocrites. That's why Jesus cleansed the Temple and why He condemned the Jews for their hypocrisy and externalism in His first great sermon, the Sermon on the Mount. Note especially what He said in Matthew 6:1-2: "Beware of practicing your righteousness before men to be noticed by them; otherwise you have no reward with your Father who is in heaven. When therefore you give alms, do not sound a trumpet before you, as the hypocrites do in the synagogues and in the streets, that they may be honored by men. Truly I say to you, they have their reward in full." Those verses capture the essence of the Jews' religion; it was mere outward show, devoid of any inner devotion to and love for God.

Sadly, those two extremes of false worship are with us today. Some worship God with their lips only, but their hearts are far from Him (cf. Isa. 29:13). Others enthusiastically promote heresy. How are we to avoid the enthusiastic heresy of Mount Gerizim and the barren orthodoxy of Jerusalem? By worshiping God in spirit and in truth. Jerusalem had the truth, but not the spirit; Mount Gerizim had the spirit, but not the truth. True worship must include both. "God is spirit," declared Jesus, "and those who worship Him must worship in spirit and truth" (John 4:24).

Worshiping God in Spirit

The term "spirit" in verse 24 does not refer to the Holy Spirit, but to the human spirit. It speaks of the inner person, the real self. True worship, Jesus says, is not a matter of externals. It's not a question of worshiping at a certain place, at a certain time, using certain rituals, or wearing certain clothing. True worship is a matter of the heart. Using a Greek word that refers especially to worshiping God, Paul wrote in Romans 1:9 that he served God in his "spirit." "Bless the LORD, O my soul," wrote David, "and all that is within me, bless His holy name" (Ps. 103:1). David's worship of God also came from deep within.

There are four basic requirements for worshiping God in spirit.

You must be spiritually alive. Apart from the new birth, no one can truly worship God, since "a natural man does not accept the things of the Spirit of God; for they are foolishness to him, and he cannot understand them, because they are spiritually appraised" (1 Cor. 2:14). Unbelievers cannot worship in spirit, because their spirits are dead in sin (Eph. 2:1-3). Thus they lack the capacity to respond to spiritual truth. The inner transformation brought about by salvation is thus a necessary prerequisite for any genuine worship. As the psalmist wrote, "Revive us, and we will call upon Thy name" (Ps. 80:18).

Your heart must be focused on God. That involves contemplating God at all times, being able to say with David, "I have set the LORD continually before me" (Ps. 16:8). Planting God's truth in your heart excites your spirit to worship. To do that you must read the Word, hear it taught, and, especially, meditate on it. "This book of the law shall not depart from your mouth," the Lord commanded Joshua, "but you shall meditate on it day and night" (Josh. 1:8). Biblical meditation differs radically from that of eastern religions. The goal of Eastern meditation is to empty the mind; the goal of biblical meditation is to fill it with God's truth. Biblical meditation may be defined as focusing your whole mind on one subject. The church has largely lost the ability for deep thinking and meditation on God's truth, and the inevitable result of such shallow thinking is shallow worship.

As you read the Bible, read it to learn more about God's character and works. Read it to know Christ better and more deeply. As you meditate deeply on its majestic truths, your spirit will rise in worship to God.

Your heart must be undivided. David prayed in Psalm 86:11-12, "Unite my heart to fear Thy name. I will give thanks to Thee, O LORD my God, with all my heart." Worship arises from an undivided, undistracted heart. That's why you can't worship God while entertaining sin in your life. "If I regard wickedness in my heart," wrote the psalmist, "the LORD will not hear" (Ps. 66:18). Jesus taught in the Sermon on the Mount that dealing with sin against others is a prerequisite for worship: "If therefore you are presenting your offering at the altar, and there remember that your brother has something against you, leave your offering there before the altar, and go your way; first be reconciled to your brother, and then come and present your offering" (Matt. 5:23-24). The Lord described wayward Israel to Ezekiel as those who "sit before you as My people, and they hear your words, but they do not do them; for with their mouth they show much love, but their hearts pursue their own gain" (Ezek. 33:31, NKJV). Their divided allegiance kept them from truly worshiping God, as did that of the Pharisees, whom Jesus warned, "You are those who justify yourselves in the sight of men, but God knows your hearts" (Luke 16:15).

If you would truly worship God, you must be constantly dealing with sin in your life.

You must be Spirit-controlled. Philippians 3:3 defines true worshipers as those who "worship in the Spirit of God." The Holy Spirit must energize our worship if it is to be acceptable. And for Him to do that, we must be Spirit-controlled people (Eph. 5:18). To be Spirit-controlled means to constantly yield to His will as revealed in the Scriptures (Col. 3:16).

What hinders us from worshiping in spirit? In a word, self. Someone totally focused on himself is not even a Christian. And Christians cannot worship God with hearts divided between themselves and Him. Nor can they be Spirit-controlled if they yield only a portion of their lives to His control. If we allow it, self will always hinder our worship. That is where the battle to maintain purity in our worship must be fought.

Worshiping God in Truth

It is self-evident that true worship must be in response to what is true about God. That's why Jesus said in John 17:17, "Sanctify them in the truth; Thy word is truth." Or, in the words of the psalmist, "Sing praises with understanding" (Ps. 47:7, NKJV). God is not honored when we conceive Him to be other than He is, when we misunderstand His attributes, works, will, and purpose.

That's why a proper understanding of God's Word is crucial.

Only by rightly interpreting the Word of truth can we gain the knowledge that is essential if we are to worship God in a way that pleases Him.

Genuine worship joins spirit and truth as our spirits soar in praise in response to the indisputable realities revealed in Scripture. There is no premium on ecstatic ignorance or indifference to doctrinal precision; nor is there any benefit in cold, joyless apprehension of the truth.

PREPARING YOUR HEART FOR WORSHIP

Hebrews 10:22 presents a concise checklist for preparing to worship God. Before you worship Him, ask yourself the following questions:

Am I sincere? "Let us draw near with a sincere heart," exhorts the writer of Hebrews. We need to ask the Lord to help us put aside all worldly distractions and focus on Him.

Am I coming in faith? We must approach God "in full assurance of faith," that is, resting fully on the sufficiency of Christ's sacrifice for our sins, not on our good deeds, to gain us access into God's presence.

Am I humble? We must have "our hearts sprinkled clean from an evil conscience." The accusations of the conscience humble us by reminding us of our sin, as does the remembrance of God's grace and mercy toward us.

Am I pure? The writer of Hebrews expressed this truth when he wrote of having "our bodies washed with pure water." We must confess and forsake our sin before coming to God in worship.

If the answer to those four questions is yes, we may draw near to God with confidence, knowing that our worship will be acceptable to Him. And the blessed truth is that when we draw near to God on His terms, He promises to draw near to us (Jas. 4:8). When all this is true of us, we'll be known as people who have a genuine attitude of worship toward the true and living God.

13

HOPE:
OUR FUTURE IS GUARANTEED

The future of mankind is a topic that seems to be on the minds of many people these days. Just look at the number of books and movies that deal with global annihilation through nuclear war, alien invasion, or natural disaster and you'll see what I mean.

Such a preoccupation fuels people with the need to develop some kind of assurance about their future—not only their mortal existence, but their immortality as well. As a result, many turn to the various religions of the world and their explanations of the future and promises for the afterlife. A growing number today are trusting in the promises of the New Age movement and its belief in reincarnation. Even those who don't adhere to any religious code or belief system hope their own righteous deeds will guarantee them a slot in some heavenly existence.

Some people hope in their ingenuity. They try to hedge against the realities of life's inevitable tragedies by amassing fortunes and spending them on medical research to not only prolong life but to cheat death. Ultimately people must put their trust in something to give themselves some assurance about their future.

Certain people, however, dismiss hope altogether and believe there is no life after death. Such a view allows them to pursue a hedonistic philosophy of life so they can live with no moral code and do whatever gives them pleasure because they believe there is no judgment of immorality.

Whether unregenerate people hold to a bleak view of the future or a bright hope for tomorrow and eternity, the fact is that they are "separate from Christ, excluded from the commonwealth of Israel, and strangers to the covenants of promise, having no hope and without God in the world" (Eph. 2:12). Anyone without God and Christ has no hope for the future. Without hope, death takes on terrifying proportions; all that is left is eternal hell, eternal pain, and eternal punishment. That's why Job 27:8 says, "For what is the hope of the hypocrite . . . when God taketh away his soul?" (KJV). Proverbs 10:28 adds, "The hope of the righteous is gladness, but the expectation of the wicked perishes."

There are only two possible destinations in eternity—heaven or hell—and God created them both. Those who are headed for heaven by faith in Jesus Christ have hope; the rest have no hope and will experience the eternal hopelessness of hell. Perhaps one of the greatest torments of hell is the knowledge that the pain will never cease. Such is the epitome of hopelessness.

A DEFINITION OF HOPE

I find it frightening to even contemplate a life without hope. Fortunately, those of us who have put our trust in Jesus Christ have reason to hope, and this is not at all as the world defines hope. Most people use hope as a synonym for "wish" or "desire." They hope someone they long to see will visit, they hope to get the job they're after, they hope to get the grades they're pursuing, they hope their dreams come to pass.

But in the Bible hope is not a wish, it is a reality—a fact not yet realized. Biblical hope is a fact that God has promised and will fulfill. As such, it represents the final pillar of Christian character. Hope is the spiritual attitude that causes us to look confidently into the future and motivates us to pursue Christlikeness with maximum effort. To see how hope is central to the believer's life of faith, let's look at several Scriptures.

Hope Is Secure

The author of Hebrews says, "This hope we have as an anchor of the soul, a hope both sure and steadfast and one which enters within the veil, where Jesus has entered as a forerunner for us" (6:19-20). Our hope is an anchor, which means it is not movable or shakeable. Our hope is embodied in Christ Himself, who has entered into God's presence in the heavenly Holy of Holies on our behalf. He serves as our great High Priest, forever interceding before God for us.

In his first epistle, the apostle Peter offers as further proof of the security of our hope:

> *Blessed be the God and Father of our Lord Jesus Christ, who according to His great mercy has caused us to be born again to a living hope through the resurrection of Jesus Christ from the dead, to obtain an inheritance which is imperishable and undefiled and will not fade away, reserved in heaven for you, who are protected by the power of God through faith for a salvation ready to be revealed in the last time. In this you greatly rejoice, even though now for a little while, if necessary, you have been distressed by various trials.*
>
> —1:3-6

Hope Is an Essential Part of the Gospel

"We give thanks to God, the Father of our Lord Jesus Christ, praying always for you, since we heard of your faith in Christ Jesus and the love you which have for all the saints; because of the hope laid up for you in heaven, of which you previously heard in the word of truth, the gospel" (Col. 1:3-5). The Gospel includes our eternal hope. The joy of our salvation is that one day we will enter into eternal life in heaven. That is a promised fact.

All three aspects of our salvation—past, present, and future—are bound up in the Gospel. In Titus 1:1-2 Paul writes, "Paul, a bond-servant of God, and an apostle of Jesus Christ, for the faith of those chosen of God and the knowledge of the truth which is according to godliness, in the hope of eternal life." Paul preached the Gospel so that the elect ("those chosen of God") could believe and be saved. That's the past aspect—our justification. Those whom God chooses hear the Gospel, believe, and therefore are justified by Him. The present aspect of the Gospel is "the knowledge of the truth which is according to godliness." That's our sanctification. The future aspect is "the hope of eternal life," which is our glorification.

In the past we were saved from the penalty of sin—we will not be condemned. We won't bear the consequences for our sins because God imputed the righteousness of Christ to us the moment we believed. Christ bore all our iniquity in His own body on the cross. In the present we are being saved from the power of sin as the Holy Spirit and the truth of the Scriptures give us victory over sin. And we will be saved from the presence of sin when sometime in the future we go to heaven. Without the promise of future glory the Gospel would be an empty promise instead of a secure fact.

Hope Makes Us Persevere

Romans 8 is a great chapter of promise for the believer. Here Paul states that God will fulfill the believer's hope and bring him to glory:

> *We ourselves groan within ourselves, waiting eagerly for our adoption as sons, the redemption of our body. For in hope we have been saved, but hope that is seen is not hope; for why does one also hope for what he sees? But if we hope for what we do not see, with perseverance we wait eagerly for it. . . . And we know that God causes all things to work together for good to those who love God, to those who are called according to His purpose. For whom He foreknew, He also predestined to become conformed to the image of His Son, that He might be the first-born among many brethren; and whom He predestined, these He also called; and whom He called, these He also justified; and whom He justified, these He also glorified.*
>
> *—vv. 23-25, 28-30*

Our hope is glory. We want to experience the redemption of our body and finally be rid of the sinful battle in our flesh. That is the one element of our salvation we have yet to realize. Even though it is future, it is promised, pledged, and guaranteed. Thus, for us glory is a fact. That's why we persevere while we wait eagerly for our glorification. No matter what trials and struggles we face while we wait, we can be sure God will fulfill His calling of us and bring us to glory. Since God made the effort to justify us, we can be sure He will also glorify us because that's His plan.

FEATURES OF HOPE

The Bible breaks down the concept of our hope into several components. Here are ten features of our hope that should produce joy in our hearts.

Our Hope Comes from God
It is essential that our hope is objective, not subjective. It is not a secular pipe dream telling you that you can be anything you want to be. You can't create or control the future—you don't have either the power or the knowledge to do so. You don't have to concoct some scheme for the future—God has already given you one. Psalm 43:5 says, "Why are you in despair, O my soul? And why are you disturbed within me? Hope in God, for I shall again praise Him, the help of my countenance, and my God." The psalmist is simply reminding us not to despair because God is the source of our hope.

Our Hope Is a Gift of Grace
Second Thessalonians 2:16-17 says, "Now may our Lord Jesus Christ Himself and God the Father, who has loved us and given us eternal comfort and good hope by grace, comfort and strengthen your hearts in every good work and word." The eternal comfort and good hope God gave is not something we deserved. God gives it to whom He will, according to His own sovereign desires.

Our Hope Is Defined by Scripture
Romans 15:4 says, "Whatever was written in earlier times was written for our instruction, that through perseverance and the encouragement of the Scriptures we might have hope." When you need

comfort and encouragement, look to God's Word because it will give you hope in the midst of all the trials of life.

Our Hope Is Reasonable

Our hope is not irrational; it isn't based on how the stars line up or on advice from the psychic network. Our hope is defined by Scripture, and that makes it reasonable. The apostle Peter said, "Sanctify Christ as Lord in your hearts, always being ready to make a defense to every one who asks you to give an account for the hope that is in you" (1 Pet. 3:15). If someone asks you what you think is going to happen to the world, you can take them to the Bible and explain God's plan for the future.

Our Hope Is Secured by Christ's Resurrection

Peter states clearly that God "has caused us to be born again to a living hope through the resurrection of Jesus Christ from the dead" (1 Pet. 1:3). Jesus Christ came back from death. More than 500 people saw Him on one occasion (1 Cor. 15:6). His own disciples communed with Him intimately after His resurrection (Luke 24:36-49; John 20:19—21:23). They ate with Him and touched Him. They saw the scars in His hands from His crucifixion. Before He was crucified, Jesus said, "Because I live, you shall live also" (John 14:19). That's our hope. He went through death and came out the other side alive, paving the way for us.

Our Hope Is Confirmed by the Holy Spirit

Romans 15:13 says, "Now may the God of hope fill you with all joy and peace in believing, that you may abound in hope by the power of the Holy Spirit." The Bible explains your hope, and when you go through some crisis, the Holy Spirit empowers you to endure. Your knowledge of Scripture works in combination with the energizing power of the Spirit to sustain you in your darkest hour, enabling you to hold on to your hope.

Our Hope Is a Defense Against Satan's Attacks

Satan wants us to doubt and question God. He attacks our minds with doubt about the reality of our salvation. But we wear the "helmet" that is "the hope of salvation" (1 Thess. 5:8). Thus we can remain secure in the knowledge of God's Word and its many promises of our eternal salvation (John 6:37-39; 10:28-29; Rom. 5:10; 8:31-39; Phil. 1:6; 1 Pet. 1:3-5). The Holy Scriptures give us the foundation on which to build our hope.

Our Hope Is Strengthened Through Trials

The more you experience trials, the more you have the opportunity to exercise your hope. And the more you exercise it, the stronger it gets, enabling you to endure even greater suffering. That's how the grace of God works. We ought to look forward to trials because they perfect us in many areas, including our hope (Jas. 1:4, 12).

As you experience more and more trials, you'll long even more for heaven. Everything I want is in heaven. As you and I get older, more of the people who are dearest to us will have gone there. Thus heaven becomes even more precious. Experience enough trials and soon you'll say with the apostle Paul, "To live is Christ, and to die is gain . . . having the desire to depart and be with Christ" (Phil. 1:21, 23).

Our Hope Produces Joy

Even in the midst of sorrow, our hope will produce joy. Psalm 146:5 connects hope with joy: "How blessed [happy] is he whose help is the God of Jacob, whose hope is in the LORD his God." When you have hope in God, you have joy.

Our Hope Will Be Fulfilled at Christ's Return

You might have thought that hope is fulfilled right after we die. But death simply gets our spirits to heaven—our bodies have yet to be raised. They await the Rapture of the church: "For the Lord Himself will descend from heaven with a shout, with the voice of the archangel, and with the trumpet of God; and the dead in Christ shall rise first.

Then we who are alive and remain shall be caught up together with them in the clouds to meet the Lord in the air, and thus we shall always be with the Lord" (1 Thess. 4:16-17). Those who are dead in Christ—whose spirits are already with the Lord—will be united with their glorified bodies. That's when our hope becomes reality.

THE PRACTICE OF HOPE

One question remains: How does our hope affect our lives right now? We need to look at 1 John 2:28—3:3 to see how the apostle John deals with the theme of hope and its daily application for believers.

As we noted in the previous section, the spirits of believers who die go directly into the presence of the Lord and live in perfect joy and righteousness. But believers are not yet complete because they have not experienced the full completion of their hope in the resurrection of their glorified bodies. John states our current situation when he says, "Beloved, now we are children of God, and it has not appeared as yet what we shall be" (3:2). We have not yet been glorified, as we will be when Christ returns. At that time those believers who are dead and those who are alive will become perfect both in the inner and outer man. Our hope will finally be fully realized.

To see just how we ought to prepare for that day, John gives us five features of the believer's hope. Here is how believers will live if they have hope.

Hope Is Guaranteed by Abiding

John writes, "Little children, abide in Him, so that when He appears, we may have confidence and not shrink away from Him in shame at His coming" (2:28). When the Lord returns, there will be two responses: the saints will welcome Him, but the ungodly will be ashamed. Revelation 6:15-16 says the ungodly will hide "themselves in the caves and among the rocks of the mountains; and they [will say] to the mountains and the rocks, 'Fall on us and hide us from the presence of Him who sits on the throne, and from the wrath of the Lamb.'"

As believers we need not hide when He comes; we can be confident because we have been abiding in Him. The notion of abiding is best defined by the picture Jesus presented when He likened Himself to the vine and to believers as the branches: "Abide in Me, and I in you. As the branch cannot bear fruit of itself, unless it abides in the vine, so neither can you, unless you abide in Me" (John 15:4).

The word "abide" basically means "to remain." It gives evidence of genuine salvation. John alluded to that when he referred to so-called believers who "went out from us, but they were not really of us; for if they had been of us, they would have remained with us; but they went out, in order that it might be shown that they all are not of us" (1 John 2:19). People with genuine faith will remain with the fellowship. They won't defect; they won't deny Christ or abandon His truth. Jesus reiterated the importance of abiding when He said to the Jews who believed in Him, "If you abide in My Word, then you are truly disciples of Mine" (John 8:31).

When the apostle John calls on believers to abide in Christ, that is in essence a call for the perseverance of the saints. He is bidding us to adhere to the Gospel, to live in constant dependence on Jesus Christ, and to render continued loving obedience to His Word.

That by no means negates God's part in securing our salvation. The Lord promises that He will never lose any of us and that He'll bring us all to glory. But such lofty privileges don't cancel our obligations to be obedient children; they increase our duty. The greater the privileges of grace, the greater our responsibility to be obedient. Paul says, "For the grace of God has appeared, bringing salvation to all men, instructing us to deny ungodliness and worldly desires and to live sensibly, righteously and godly in the present age" (Titus 2:11-12).

When we remain faithful to abide in Christ by maintaining our obedience, that guarantees our hope. You have a responsibility before God to persevere in faith and faithfulness, to daily express your loving obedience to the Word of God and the purposes of God as they unfold in your life. Paul lived with that attitude and could say as his life came to a close: "I have fought the good fight, I have finished the course, I have kept the faith; in the future there is laid up for me the crown of righteousness, which the Lord, the righteous Judge, will award to me on that day; and not only to me, but also to all who have loved His appearing" (2 Tim. 4:7-8). Paul did not waver from sound doctrine or his trust in God. As a result, he had confidence about meeting the Lord. You and I are obligated to remain faithful to the Lord, just as Paul did.

Hope Is Realized in Righteousness

You guarantee your future hope by abiding, and abiding is just another way of describing righteous living. John says, "If you know that He is righteous, you know that every one also who practices righteousness is born of Him" (1 John 2:29). Our hope must result in righteous behavior. People who hope to be righteous when the Lord appears must be manifesting righteousness now.

A Christian reveals his true character by his fruits. A person can claim any kind of allegiance to Christianity he wants, but what is the pattern of his life? Just as a natural child will be like his father, so the children of God will be like their heavenly Father. Since God is righteous, His children will reflect His righteous nature. Jesus said, "Therefore you are to be perfect, as your heavenly Father is perfect" (Matt. 5:48). That is the goal we pursue.

The verb "practices righteousness" in 1 John 2:29 is a present indicative, which means it has continuous action. Thus a true believer who has genuine hope and abides in Christ will practice righteousness in his life. He has "put on the new self, which in the likeness of God has been created in righteousness and holiness of the truth" (Eph. 4:24).

It is important to examine your works. To affirm your hope, ask yourself, *What do I believe?* Then ask, *What is my life like?* If you don't have a passion and desire for righteousness, then it's doubtful that you're a Christian.

Hope Is Established in Love

John writes, "See how great a love the Father has bestowed upon us, that we should be called children of God" (1 John 3:1). We share John's astonishment as he contemplates the amazing love of God, which confers such incredible honor on us sinners and makes us children in His family. John 1:12 says, "But as many as received Him, to them He gave the right to become children of God, even to those who believe in His name." Being God's own children is an overwhelming expression of His great love.

The phrase "how great a love" in 1 John 3:1 refers to something foreign. The love God has shown us is foreign to anything we can conceive, foreign to anything we can imagine, and foreign to anything known to the human race. Later in the epistle John says, "By this the love of God was manifested in us, that God has sent His only begotten Son into the world so that we might live through Him" (4:9). Such transcendent love, which motivated the perfect Son of God to sacrifice Himself to redeem us, is the basis of our hope. And it is "for this reason the world does not know us, because it did not know Him" (3:1). The world can't comprehend God's love because it can't understand the Gospel.

Hope Is Fulfilled in Christlikeness

John continues, "Beloved, now we are children of God, and it has not appeared as yet what we shall be. We know that, when He appears, we shall be like Him, because we shall see Him just as He is" (v. 2). Our hope is not yet fully realized. Titus 2:13 reiterates that we are "looking for the blessed hope and the appearing of the glory of our great God and Savior, Christ Jesus." When Christ returns, our hope will be fulfilled.

Remember that God has "predestined [us] to be conformed to the image of His Son, that He might be the first-born [first in pre-eminence] among many brethren" (Rom. 8:29). God's plan is to redeem His elect and make them like His Son. When Jesus returns to rapture the church, we'll see the fulfillment of that design when we become like Jesus Christ.

Paul reminds us of our goal in this life: "I press on toward the goal for the prize of the upward call of God in Christ Jesus" (Phil. 3:14). Both the goal and the prize is Christlikeness. The goal of our salvation is Christlikeness, the fulfillment of our hope is

Christlikeness, and the pursuit of our life is to be more and more like Christ.

Hope Is Guaranteed by Purity

John concludes this section when he says, "Everyone who has this hope fixed on Him purifies himself, just as He is pure" (1 John 3:3). When you live with the goal of meeting Jesus Christ face to face, that will have a purifying effect on your life. When you meet Him, He will evaluate your work and then reward you (1 Cor. 3:10-15). But it's possible you could lose your reward, so "watch yourselves, that you might not lose what we have accomplished, but that you may receive a full reward" (2 John 8).

I know our Lord could return at any time, so my goal has been to live in such a way that when I face Him I can offer Him my pure life. That goal had its origin when I was a young child and read the following poem my grandfather kept in his Bible:

> *When I stand at the judgment seat of Christ,*
> *And He shows me His plan for me,*
> *The plan of my life as it might have been,*
> *And I see how I blocked Him here and checked Him there*
> *And would not yield my will,*
> *Will there be grief in my Savior's eyes,*
> *Grief though He loves me still?*
> *He would have me rich but I stand there poor,*
> *Stripped of all but His grace,*
> *While memory runs like a haunted thing*
> *Down a path I can't retrace.*
> *Then my desolate heart will well nigh break;*
> *With tears I cannot shed,*
> *I will cover my face with my empty hands,*
> *I will bow my uncrowned head.*
> *O Lord, of the years that are left of me,*
> *I give them to Thy hand.*
> *Take me, break me, and mold me*
> *To the pattern that Thou hast planned.*

The emotions I feel now are similar to what the poet must have thought when he wrote those words. I don't want to have any reason to be ashamed at Christ's coming. I want to be doing that which honors and pleases Him. I want to be living a pure life. If your focus is on Jesus Christ, you will live a pure life and will be able to say with the apostle John, "Come, Lord Jesus" (Rev. 22:20).

The Thessalonian church was a great church. When Paul wrote to its members, he never reprimanded them; he just instructed and commended them. One of his commendations was this: "We give thanks to God always for all of you, making mention of you in our prayers; constantly bearing in mind your work of faith and labor of love and steadfastness of hope . . . [knowing you] wait for His Son from heaven" (1 Thess. 1:2-3, 10). Are you in that waiting mode? Are you living as if Jesus could come in the next moment? Are you living in such a way that if He did come you would be pleased to have Him examine your life? You need to live every moment as if He might be here the next, for He might do just that.

That then is our hope. It should not frighten us. Rather, it should fill our hearts with joy.

If you are building your life upon the pillars of Christian character we have studied throughout this book, you will not be ashamed when Jesus returns—you will be confident.

STUDY GUIDE

CHAPTER 1:
THE STARTING POINT: GENUINE FAITH

Summarizing the Chapter
For the believer, faith begins at salvation and shapes everything else in his life from then on.

Getting Started (Choose One)
1. Recall a time when your faith in a person or product was really tested. What most challenged your basic trust during the situation? Did your trust need to be restored? If so, how did that occur?
2. Do you believe that most professing Christians today truly understand the biblical definition of faith? Why or why not?

Answering the Questions
1. According to *The Baptist Confession of Faith*, what are the major elements that constitute biblical faith?
2. When did Habakkuk minister to Judah? What was the basic situation he faced?
3. What had Habakkuk likely petitioned God to do?
4. Who were the Chaldeans? Why was Habakkuk so upset that God would use them to punish Judah?
5. What great truth about God was Habakkuk reminded of? How did that help him resolve his theological dilemma?
6. What did Martin Luther's discovery of Habakkuk 2:4 result in?
7. What New Testament verses reiterate Habakkuk 2:4's key truth?
8. How did Habakkuk's use of agricultural terminology drive home his point about God's person and plan?
9. Who ultimately supplies the means for our life of faith? Give at least two verses to support your answer.

Focusing on Prayer

    • Pray that God would improve your trust and understanding of who He is and what He wants you to do as you face perplexing life situations.

    • Thank God for the means He has provided, mainly through His Word, for you to exercise genuine faith.

Applying the Truth

Read through Romans 5:1-10 every day during the coming week. Meditate on a different verse or verses each day, and write down how the important words and key principles relate to living by faith daily.

CHAPTER 2:
OBEDIENCE: THE BELIEVER'S COVENANT

Summarizing the Chapter

For Christians, faith and obedience are inseparably linked in our covenant relationship with God the Father, made possible by the shed blood of Christ the Son.

Getting Started (Choose One)

1. What basic stories and images come to mind when you think of the Old Testament? Excluding Psalms and Proverbs, how relevant has it been for your Christian life? How often do you read and study the Old Testament?

2. Have you ever been in a contractual dispute with someone? If so, how important to you was the other party's adherence to the terms of the contract? Do you believe most people today still take the terms of business and legal agreements as seriously as in previous generations? Discuss.

Answering the Questions

1. What is so foundational about the Great Commission (Matt. 28:19-20)?

2. What truth does the apostle John state at least three times? Cite one of the references.

3. How was the gospel message always preached in the New Testament? Give three examples.

4. What is the correct meaning of the scriptural term *foreknowledge*? What incorrect meaning is often given to it?
5. When does our sanctification begin, and what does it include (see John 3:5; 1 Pet. 1:2)?
6. Summarize the future phase of salvation, as stated in Ephesians 2:10.
7. What important activity was Moses engaged in just prior to the events of Exodus 24:3-8?
8. What basic promise did God make in the Mosaic law? As a result, what did His people agree to do?
9. What physical feature of Moses' altar represented the people's participation in the covenant?
10. What was the significance of the animal sacrifices and the animals' blood?
11. How can salvation be summarized as a covenant of obedience (see Jer. 31:33; Ezek. 36:26-27)?
12. What does Romans 6:16-18 illustrate as the overriding attitude and desire of all genuine Christians?
13. What happens to anyone who does not regularly apply Scripture to his life (see Jas. 1:22-25)?

Focusing on Prayer

• Spend some extra time in prayer this week thanking and praising God that He graciously foreknew you and made you a part of His family.

• Pray for an area of your Christian walk in which you need greater obedience. Ask the Lord to give you as great a resolve to obey as the Israelites had after hearing Moses.

Applying the Truth

Memorize either Matthew 28:19-20 or James 1:25. After you memorize the passage, write out your own paraphrase and share it with a friend.

CHAPTER 3:
BLESSED ARE THE HUMBLE

Summarizing the Chapter

True humility, as taught and exemplified by Jesus and Paul, is the centerpiece of the Christian life and, when practiced, will result in genuine blessing.

Getting Started (Choose One)

1. The scribes and Pharisees of Jesus' day were not noted for their humility. What group or category of people in today's society reminds you most of them? Why?

2. When is it most difficult for you to manifest humility? Relate a story from your personal experience that will illustrate your answer.

Answering the Questions

1. To what does the Greek term translated "poor" in Matthew 5:3 refer? How dependent were such people?

2. What sorts of things do people count on to get them into the kingdom of God? List at least five.

3. What does the improper kind of mourning often stem from?

4. How many different Greek words are used in the New Testament for *sorrow*? What is distinctive about the one in Matthew 5:4?

5. What does the word *gentleness* usually imply today? How is that a misunderstanding of its scriptural usage?

6. How did Jesus demonstrate true gentleness? Give some examples from His ministry.

7. What is the promised result of gentleness? What are the ramifications of that?

8. How much significance does commentator Martyn Lloyd-Jones attach to Matthew 5:6 (see the quote from his book)?

9. What should be the nature of the believer's hunger and thirst for righteousness? Why (see Phil. 1:9-10)?

10. According to Matthew 5:6, how inclusive will our desire for righteousness be? What in the Greek makes that righteousness special?

11. What was the real point of Paul's sharing his experience about being transported to heaven (2 Cor. 12:1-4)?

12. What was Paul's thorn in the flesh?

13. What are two basic marks of the humble person (see Phil. 2:3-4)?

Focusing on Prayer

• Ask for the Lord's help as you work on an area in your life in which you need to show more humility.

• Pray that today God would give you a greater hunger and thirst for His Word and righteousness.

Applying the Truth
Read chapter 4, 5, 6, 7, or 8 in Martyn Lloyd-Jones' first volume of *Studies in the Sermon on the Mount* (Grand Rapids, Mich.: Eerdmans, 1971). Take notes on the chapter you read, and look up all the Scripture references. Choose one or two new truths to meditate on and apply. (Each chapter is about ten pages long.)

CHAPTER 4:
THE SELFLESS NATURE OF LOVE

Summarizing the Chapter
The only way today's self-centered, sex-oriented culture will see genuine biblical love is if believers obey Christ's teaching and emulate His self-sacrificing example of love in John 13.

Getting Started (Choose One)
1. Can you remember the first time you "fell in love"? Were you really in love, or was it infatuation? How is infatuation different from love?
2. Where does the culture war challenge you most directly? What practical means have you found to combat the influences of worldly culture? Discuss one of them with your group.

Answering the Questions
1. What English word comes from the Greek word translated "imitators" (Eph. 5:1)?
2. What should be an instinctive inclination if we are true children of God?
3. Give a brief definition of *agapē* love.
4. What characterizes conditional human love? How is it different from God's type of love?
5. How does Satan counterfeit biblical love?
6. Immorality and impurity are both expressions of what sinful trait? What are some additional characteristics of it?
7. What is the real reason people want to have the availability of abortion?
8. What is Satan's sixfold outline in waging a culture war against God's kingdom?

9. What is the devil's primary tool for making it easier for people in society to be bad?

10. What is one of the primary distractions that has diverted western society's attention away from the sinful effects of the sexual revolution?

11. What negative factors made the disciples unlovable by human standards as the events in John 13 opened?

12. Why was foot washing necessary in the ancient Middle East, and who normally performed the task?

13. What is the meaning of Jesus' statement in John 13:8?

14. How does John 13:10 shed further light on the significance of Jesus' washing the disciples' feet? How does the verse apply to us?

15. In one sentence, how can we apply Jesus' instruction in John 13:34-35?

Focusing on Prayer

• Give thanks to God this week for His ultimate act of sacrificial love in sending Christ to die for you.

• Pray that people would be saved out of our sinful culture because of the loving influence of believers.

Applying the Truth

Pray for the salvation of an unbelieving friend, neighbor, coworker, or relative. Then reach out to the person with some practical act of love and service. If you have no close relationship with an unsaved person, look for a way to help another Christian who may need encouragement right now.

CHAPTER 5:
UNITY: PERSEVERANCE IN THE TRUTH

Summarizing the Chapter

Because it has always been God's will that the Body of Christ be united through the indwelling Spirit, based on the essential doctrines of Scripture, it is imperative that Christians maintain that unity before the unbelieving world.

Getting Started (Choose One)

1. How does a lack of unity affect morale in the workplace or on an athletic team? Have you ever witnessed such negative effects firsthand? If so, what did you learn from the experience?

2. What basic doctrines should all Christians agree on as essential? What views or practices allow for differences or individual preference? Support your answers.

Answering the Questions

1. How seriously are believers to pursue the matter of unity (Eph. 4:3)? What does the Greek in that passage indicate?
2. What kind of unity is Paul speaking of, and how is it held together (1 Cor. 12:13, 20; Col. 3:14)?
3. Who indwells every believer? What is guaranteed as a result (Rev. 19:9)?
4. What is "the faith" referred to in Jude 3?
5. What was the common New Testament way of publicly confessing one's faith in Christ?
6. What does Deuteronomy 6:4 teach about the nature of God? What references in the New Testament support that truth?
7. What two general tendencies within today's church threaten to undermine the purity of its unity?
8. What is the larger context of Jesus' statement in John 17:21? What was the real thrust of His prayer?
9. If unity is not something Christians need to manufacture, then how should we understand our role regarding it (see 1 Cor. 1:10; 2 Pet. 1:1)?
10. How does Matthew 5:48 help us see the attainability of perfect unity for the local church?
11. How does the KJV translation of 1 Corinthians 1:10 help us better understand the meaning of spiritual agreement and doctrinal unity?
12. Give several definitions, both specific and general, of the New Testament word for *divisions* (see John 7:43; 1 Cor. 1:10).
13. What is one of the most important ways a local church can prevent major divisiveness?
14. Does local church unity mean unanimity on absolutely every little issue? If not, explain your answer further.
15. What does Paul's use of the phrase "of the same mind" in Romans 15:5 say about the nature of our faith? What bearing does that have on Christian unity?

Focusing on Prayer

• Pray that the deacons and elders in your church would stay in the Word faithfully and make wise leadership decisions in order to strengthen the church's unity.

• Ask the Lord to give you the same diligent concern for unity that Jesus and Paul had. Pray that in every situation you will contribute to authentic biblical unity among other believers.

Applying the Truth

Read and study the book of Nehemiah over the next month. Notice especially the various ways and occasions that Nehemiah promoted unity and solidarity among the people. Make a list of these, and choose one that you can meditate on. Then think through its application to your own ministry.

CHAPTER 6:
GROWTH: NO REAL LIFE WITHOUT IT

Summarizing the Chapter

All genuine Christians will be growing spiritually, though at different levels of maturity. They will know that God's Word is the basis for true growth and will therefore desire to know it better and better.

Getting Started (Choose One)

1. What is your favorite hobby or leisure activity? How much time do you devote to improving your efficiency and skill in it? Is that appropriate and balanced? Why or why not? What does your spouse think? Your friends?
2. Some people will take extraordinary measures to treat a sick pet or rejuvenate a dying plant or tree. Have you known anyone like that? If so, briefly relate his or her story to the group. What is the most you would be willing to do and spend in such a case?

Answering the Questions

1. What does Scripture say about the necessity of spiritual growth? Cite two or three references.
2. *True or False*: The Bible implies there is no middle ground concerning spiritual growth; it is either present or absent from a believer's life.
3. What price do we inevitably pay for spiritual regression?
4. What term of endearment in 1 John 2 can be applied to all true believers?

5. What mature trait is lacking in all spiritual infants? What are they therefore vulnerable to?
6. What sort of spiritual warfare is Satan primarily engaged in (see 2 Cor. 10:3-5)?
7. What should be true in your life once you reach the maturity level of the spiritual young man?
8. What is the primary difference in maturity between the spiritual young man and the spiritual father?
9. In our churches today, what attitude is challenging the thoughtful, accurate understanding of Scripture?
10. What is the most succinct yet thorough passage on the importance and spiritually transforming power of Scripture?
11. How do the words of Scripture work in leading someone to salvation (John 5:24, 39; Rom. 10:17)?
12. Elaborate on the meaning of the phrase "profitable for teaching" (2 Tim. 3:16). What are its results in the life of the believer?
13. What two areas does Scripture confront as it reproves? Why is reproof so helpful (see Prov. 6:23)?
14. What positive counterpart does the Word provide to its more negative role of reproof? Explain.
15. What are the practical outworkings of Scripture's training in righteousness?
16. How does the Greek meaning of the expression "long for" (1 Pet. 2:2) help us better understand how we ought to desire God's Word?

Focusing on Prayer
• If you know of someone who is struggling with an aspect of spiritual growth, pray for that person, and ask the Lord how He might use you to help your friend.
• Ask God to increase your desire to know His Word and to grow. Pray about two or three specific areas in which you need improvement.

Applying the Truth
One way to keep track of your personal spiritual growth is with a spiritual journal. If you don't already do so, begin maintaining one this week. Start by recording insights from your devotional times and by listing prayer requests and answers to them. (For additional help on keeping a journal, see Donald S. Whitney, *Spiritual Disciplines for the Christian Life* [Colorado Springs, Colo.: NavPress, 1991], 195-211.)

CHAPTER 7:
FORGIVE AND BE BLESSED

Summarizing the Chapter

We will never exhibit a more godlike character than when we obey God's command to forgive the offenses of other believers, just as God has forgiven our offenses against Him.

Getting Started (Choose One)

1. What sort of ordinary behavior by other people makes you most irritated or impatient? Why? What is your normal reaction? How should that change or improve?

2. Other than your conversion, what time in your life do you best remember when someone extended much forgiveness, mercy, or grace to you? Describe what happened, and tell why you picked this example.

Answering the Questions

1. How did Paul identify himself in Romans 7:24 and 1 Timothy 1:15?

2. What do the Psalms and the major prophets say about God's forgiveness? Cite at least four references.

3. How is the prodigal son an example of many young men today? What did he expect from his father?

4. How is the father-son encounter in the Parable of the Prodigal Son analogous to the encounter God has with repentant sinners?

5. What does the enormous debt in Matthew 18:24 represent?

6. How do unbelievers misuse and waste their stewardship of life?

7. Why (or why not) and how should (or should not) all sinners respond as the first slave did in Matthew 18:23-35?

8. How might the Lord discipline us if we are unforgiving? How is that related to Matthew 18's lesson?

9. What balanced mix of attitudes does real forgiveness involve regarding the sins of others?

10. What sorts of blessings from God does an unforgiving Christian forfeit?

Focusing on Prayer

• Set aside some time to examine your heart and see if you possess the proper attitude of forgiveness toward fellow believers. If the Lord reveals some shortcomings, ask His forgiveness and pray that you might correct them.

• Thank God that His generous and merciful forgiveness of sins for all believers includes you.

Applying the Truth

Depending on what's most applicable and profitable for your current situation, commit either Psalm 32:1-2 or Ephesians 4:32 to memory.

CHAPTER 8:
REASON ENOUGH TO REJOICE

Summarizing the Chapter

Believers are commanded to have God's true joy at all times and in every situation.

Getting Started (Choose One)

1. Share your favorite "comfort food." Why did you pick that one? Is it one you have when celebrating a special event?
2. What was the happiest occasion you can remember before you were a Christian? Since you came to the Lord? What was the biggest difference in your appreciation of the two events? Explain.

Answering the Questions

1. What is implicit in the dictionary definition of the word *joy*?
2. What is always true of joy according to the many Greek words used for it in the New Testament?
3. What do Philippians 4:4 and 1 Thessalonians 5:16 both say about joy?
4. In light of the many Scripture texts on joy, what should be true of the Christian in regard to life's difficulties?
5. Why should times of trial make us happier than when times are easy? Support your answer with Scripture.
6. Is there a place for the outward emotions of sorrow and sadness? How should they relate to inward joy?
7. Why is the world's joy so inadequate (Prov. 14:12-13; Eccles. 2:10-11)?
8. What is the only circumstance in life that should diminish our true joy?
9. What characteristics of God give us reason for joy in the first place?

10. Give two New Testament references that present reasons for our rejoicing in Christ's redemptive work.

11. State three reasons, with supporting Scriptures, why we can have joyful confidence in the Holy Spirit's work.

12. What kinds of things demonstrate God's continual blessings to believers?

13. Give a brief definition of divine providence.

14. What general characteristic of God's Word should keep us from ever abandoning our God-given joy?

15. How do false expectations and pride rob us of true joy?

16. What is the main reason believers lack true joy?

17. What was the significance of the regular greeting between believers in the early church? How might such a greeting be helpful for today's Christians?

Focusing on Prayer

• Spend some extra prayer time this week simply rejoicing and thanking God for all the truths about joy you learned in this chapter.

• Look back over the list of reasons for a lack of joy. Pick out one or two that apply to your life, and pray that God would help you overcome those sins.

Applying the Truth

Read John MacArthur's book *The Glory of Heaven* (Wheaton, Ill.: Crossway Books, 1996). As you read, underline key thoughts and make marginal notes or take notes in a notebook. Look especially for insights on how you might transfer your focus from the temporary cares of this life to the joyful prospect of eternity with God. When you're finished reading, write out what was most helpful to you and how it will change your attitudes and actions.

CHAPTER 9:
ALWAYS A PLACE FOR GRATITUDE

Summarizing the Chapter

Because gratitude is commanded and God is displeased when it's absent, Christians must obey His Word and express thanks for all things, in all circumstances.

Getting Started (Choose One)

1. Name something that you find easy to be thankful for (excluding obvious things such as salvation, spouse, or children). Why did you choose that one? In contrast, what do you find difficult to be grateful for? Explain and discuss.

2. Do you think it's as easy today for people to be content as it was forty or fifty years ago? Why or why not? If you feel they're not as content, what do you hear at your workplace or in the marketplace as a frequent complaint?

Answering the Questions

1. Why is it so remarkable that the only one of the cleansed lepers (Luke 17:11-19) who gave thanks was a Samaritan?

2. Where does ingratitude rank among God's list of damning sins in Romans 1:18-32?

3. What are three ways the average unbeliever responds to the circumstances in his life?

4. Elements of what Old Testament offerings are combined when we observe the Lord's Table?

5. How does accepting God's sovereignty help us to express gratitude in every situation?

6. What is the ultimate object of all our gratitude? Cite several Scripture references that support your answer.

7. In the context of 2 Corinthians 9:8-15, how is believers' gratitude multiplied?

8. What are the seven hindrances to gratitude that this chapter listed? Which ones most specifically are the same as the hindrances to joy?

9. What is ideally portrayed by Paul in Philippians 4:11-12?

10. As Paul wrote his letter to the Philippians, how did his circumstances challenge him?

11. Taking into consideration the Greek usage, define the expressions "content" and "learned the secret" (Phil. 4:11-12).

12. What truths about God from the Old Testament supported Paul's attitude of contentment?

13. What additional guidelines did Paul express in his own writings that shaped his contentment?

Focusing on Prayer
- Spend a portion of your prayer time thanking the Lord for something extra-special He has done in your life recently.
- Review the list of hindrances to gratitude. Pick one that has been a difficult challenge for you, and pray that God would enable you to overcome it. (You may choose a related hindrance that is not on the list.)

Applying the Truth

Compile a list of reasons for having an attitude of thankfulness. This should apply to you specifically and to all Christians generally. Fortify your list with as many Scripture references as you can. This list could be an ongoing section of your spiritual journal (or, if you didn't begin a journal, a separate list that you refer to periodically) that regularly helps motivate you to stay grateful.

CHAPTER 10:
THE COURAGE TO BE STRONG

Summarizing the Chapter

Spiritual strength is the courage to uncompromisingly live out one's Christian convictions, which are derived from the Word of God and are best exemplified in the portraits of the spiritual teacher, soldier, athlete, and farmer.

Getting Started (Choose One)

1. If the choice were entirely up to you, would you prefer to live on a farm or in the city? What advantages and disadvantages are there to each setting? If you have lived on a farm (or ranch) or had an extended visit to one, relate to your study group what you most appreciated about farming/ranching.
2. An interesting question that has circulated in recent years is, "Are you a morning person or an evening person?" How would you answer that? Do you feel your daily schedule is structured to maximize your best time of day? How, if at all, does this issue relate to spiritual strength? Discuss.

Answering the Questions

1. What is the more literal translation of "act like men" in 1 Corinthians 16:13, and how does that clarify the expression's meaning?

2. Cite four Old Testament passages that illustrate the concept of strength and courage.
3. What must be true in our lives if we are to fulfill the command to be spiritually strong (see Eph. 3:14-16)?
4. Why did Paul value Timothy's help so much with the church at Ephesus? What was happening there?
5. What led to Timothy's being affected by the problems at Ephesus? What temporary impact did that have on his effectiveness in ministry?
6. What twofold benefit results for those who teach others?
7. Give the four reasons that preparation helps the teacher personally.
8. What has the world system implemented that justifies believers' engaging in spiritual warfare?
9. How is being a soldier for Christ analogous to being a soldier in the secular realm?
10. What specific goal should motivate us to compete hard for victory as athletes for Christ?
11. Give several examples from secular sports of why we need to compete according to the rules. What does Paul say?
12. What is the most fascinating and perhaps most important thing not said in the Parable of the Soils (Matt. 13:3-23)?
13. What is the moral of the Parable of the Soils, and how does it relate to being a spiritual farmer?
14. Which of the four images of the strong Christian best fits most Christians most of the time?

Focusing on Prayer

• Pray for your local church, and the church around the world, that members and leaders would hold strong doctrinal convictions and live by scriptural principles in everything.

• Look one more time at the four portraits of the strong Christian, and identify two or three characteristics from them in which you are weak. Ask God to help you strengthen your life in specific ways in those areas.

Applying the Truth

Commit 1 Kings 2:2-3 or 1 Corinthians 15:58 to memory. For a more challenging assignment, you might want to memorize Joshua 1:5-9 over the next few weeks. Whichever passage you choose, review it with another believer, to keep yourself accountable.

CHAPTER 11:
SELF-DISCIPLINE: THE KEY TO VICTORY

Summarizing the Chapter

Self-discipline is an essential key to spiritual growth; therefore, Christians are to pursue it diligently.

Getting Started (Choose One)

1. Think of a time when you participated in a sport. What sacrifices were required of you? What motivated you to make them? How did the level of your self-discipline affect your performance?
2. Name a person whose commitment to God has been an example to you. (This can be either someone you know personally or a person from church history.) Briefly discuss why you chose him or her.

Answering the Questions

1. Why does the Bible use athletic metaphors to picture the Christian life?
2. Give both a practical and a biblical definition of self-discipline.
3. Explain why self-discipline is necessary to master any endeavor in life.
4. Why is self-discipline in the seemingly insignificant issues of life important? Why are there are no small issues involving a person's integrity?
5. Explain the relationship between correction and self-discipline.
6. List some biblical thought guidelines that will help you be sober in spirit.
7. What two elements are common to all of the biblical principles for self-discipline?
8. Why is God the rightful owner of all men? Of believers particularly?
9. What is man's part in the covenant of salvation?
10. Explain why sin involves more than merely breaking God's law.
11. Trace the origin and development of our sinful acts.
12. How can we win the battle against the temptations that assault our imaginations?

Focusing on Prayer

• Meditate on the price God paid to redeem you. Thank Him for your salvation, and resolve to discipline yourself for godliness (1 Tim. 4:7) so you can serve Him more effectively.

• Pray that God would help you win the battle against temptation in your imagination. Ask Him to give you victory over secret sins as you faithfully study and meditate on His Word.

Applying the Truth

Go over the list of practical steps for developing self-discipline listed in the chapter, and identify your strengths and weaknesses. Make a commitment to begin working on your weaknesses, and ask someone to hold you accountable.

CHAPTER 12:
WORSHIPING GOD IN SPIRIT AND IN TRUTH

Summarizing the Chapter

To worship God in spirit and in truth is the believer's responsibility, privilege, and highest calling.

Getting Started (Choose One)

1. Describe a situation in which giving in to the tyranny of the urgent hurt you in the long run. What since then has helped you focus more on what's important?
2. What are some of the biggest threats facing the church today? Where does the issue of improper worship rank? Discuss your answer.

Answering the Questions

1. Why is worship being de-emphasized in today's church?
2. What's wrong with aiming the church service at unbelievers? Should the church seek to make unbelievers feel comfortable? Why or why not?
3. Give a biblical definition of a Christian who relates to worship.
4. Are worship and serving God mutually exclusive? Explain your answer.
5. Give a definition of worship. Is it merely an attitude, or can it be expressed in actions? Support your answer from Scripture.

6. How does a person become a true worshiper of God?
7. List the five elements that summarize the plan of redemption in the Old Testament.
8. What two realities about God are essential to true worship?
9. Why is God not to be represented by material objects?
10. Describe the two extremes of false worship represented by the Jews and Samaritans of Jesus' day.
11. What does it mean to worship God in spirit?
12. List four requirements for worshiping God in spirit.
13. What is the main hindrance to worshiping God in spirit?
14. How do we worship God in truth?

Focusing on Prayer
• Scripture reveals many of God's attributes, such as His power, wisdom, mercy, sovereignty, and love. Choose one or more of His attributes, and spend time praising Him for them.
• The biblical writers frequently praise God for His mighty works of creation, deliverance, and redemption. Think of something God has done, either from Scripture or your own life, and spend time thanking and praising Him for it.

Applying the Truth
As noted in the chapter, meditating on Scripture is an important element of true worship. Read the following passages, and list the various things upon which the psalmists meditated: Psalm 1:1-2; 63:6; 77:12; 119:15, 27, 48, 97-105; 143:5. Make them the subjects of your own meditation.

CHAPTER 13:
HOPE: OUR FUTURE IS GUARANTEED

Summarizing the Chapter
Biblical hope is an essential, factual part of our salvation—past, present, and future—that God promises through His Word and that motivates our sanctification as we daily seek to be more Christlike.

Getting Started (Choose One)
1. How did you define *hope* when you were a child? What were the most

common things you placed your hope in? Were most of those hopes fulfilled? How? Which ones weren't?

2. What, other than uncertainty about death, do you think threatens the average unsaved person's sense of hope the most? Discuss two or three possibilities. Do you encounter these very often during a typical week? If so, how?

Answering the Questions

1. What are the only two possible eternal destinations for people? How does that affect hope? Cite several verses.
2. What is the characteristic and embodiment of hope as stated in Hebrews 6:19-20?
3. What are the three aspects of salvation? (Each one includes both a time reference and a corresponding doctrinal term.) Cite Scriptures that will support your answer.
4. Is hope objective or subjective? Bolster your answer with God's Word.
5. What historical details in the New Testament, related to Christ's resurrection, strengthen the believer's hope?
6. What does the Holy Spirit do to help you sustain genuine hope?
7. What category of life experiences, encountered more and more frequently, ought to make us long for heaven?
8. What analogy, presented by Christ, best describes the concept of abiding? What is the basic definition and purpose for our abiding? Give at least two Scripture references.
9. How does a Christian reveal his true character (1 John 2:29)?
10. What is the goal and prize of the believer's earthly life (Phil. 3:14; Titus 2:13)?
11. What effect does the ultimate goal of the Christian life have on our current lives (1 John 3:2-3)? What added incentive is present (1 Cor. 3:10-15; 2 John 8)?

Focusing on Prayer

• Thank God that through His Word and His Son He has provided many solid reasons for you to have true hope.

• Pray for a non-Christian friend or a Christian friend who is struggling with assurance, that he might, by God's grace and mercy, receive new or renewed hope.

Applying the Truth

Read Revelation 21—22, and focus on the glorious future that awaits every believer. List all the things in this passage that ought to be sources of hope and joy. Meditate at length on several items from your list, and jot down additional insights the Lord gives you. Notice also the warnings near the end of chapter 22. How should these be incentives to holy living?

SCRIPTURE
INDEX

GENERAL
INDEX